M000033676

Rebuilding Trust in Healthcare

Rebuilding Trust in Healthcare

A Doctor's Prescription for a Post-Pandemic America

Paul Pender, MD

EARLY ARRIVAL PRESS
NEW HAMPSHIRE

Rebuilding Trust in Healthcare:
A Doctor's Prescription for a Post-Pandemic America

Paul Pender, MD

ISBN:978-0-578-75596-0

Library of Congress Control Number: 2020916599

©2020 Paul Pender, MD
All rights reserved.

No part of this publication may be reproduced,
stored in a retrieval system, or transmitted in any form or
by any means, electronic, mechanical, photocopying, recording,
or otherwise without prior permission.

Disclaimers: Although the author and publisher have made every effort to ensure that the information in this book was correct at press time, the author and publisher do not assume and hereby disclaim any liability to any party for any loss, damage, or disruption caused by errors or omissions, whether such errors or omissions result from negligence, accident, or any other cause. This book is not intended to provide any medical advice. The reader should consult a physician in matters relating to health and particularly with respect to any symptoms that may require diagnosis or medical attention.

EARLY ARRIVAL PRESS
NEW HAMPSHIRE

Praise for *Rebuilding Trust*

"The cornerstone of healthcare, the relationship between a doctor and a patient, is under attack. Hospitals want patients to self-identify as being a patient of the hospital, and insurance companies want patients to identify with them. But neither hospitals nor health insurers actually care for patients—doctors care for patients. Fortunately for patients in America, people like Dr. Paul Pender are fighting back. Using his experience of a long and satisfying career, and a sometimes light and humorous touch, Dr. Pender outlines the consequences of losing that crucial, therapeutic relationship. Both doctors and patients become marginalized in the pursuit of profits and consolidation. There are solutions, and Dr. Pender suggests a good place to start."

—Barbara L. McAneny, MD, MACP, FASCO
AMA Past President, CEO New Mexico Oncology
Hematology Consultants, Ltd.

"Dr. Paul Pender's new book, *Rebuilding Trust in Healthcare: A Doctor's Prescription for a Post-Pandemic America*, examines the state of healthcare delivery in the US with the refreshing honesty of a seasoned practitioner who has observed firsthand the erosion of the doctor-patient relationship over the past 38 years. His critique is unfailingly objective and avoids even a hint of political bias. The message he sends is simple: both the patient and physician have suffered from the deterioration of the sacred connection they once shared. His analysis of where the damage was inflicted is spot-on, and his ideas for damage control and restoration are well conceived and thoughtfully articulated. But I think what I liked most about this book is simply that its language and message are fully accessible to both physician and patient alike. If we are to rebuild trust in our healthcare system, it will require the effort of both the healer and the patient. Dr. Pender has given us the blueprint. The rest is up to us."

–Randall Cook, MD, FACS
Host of the podcast Rx for Success

"Where other contemporary authors have been content to simply detail and decry the problem, Dr. Pender has courageously and competently outlined a solution for rebuilding trust in today's healthcare system: Make the foundational block of that system the patient-physician partnership. From there, solutions will organically grow. Drawing upon up-to-date research and current medical topics, Dr. Pender outlines steps that medical professionals and all healthcare providers can take together to create a new medical model that will benefit both patients and providers. This book offers a timely and hopeful strategy for the future of healthcare!"

–Shirley Field, MSEd Psy

"The US healthcare system may not be entirely broken but it is, indeed, severely dysfunctional. It is fragmented, expensive, insufficient, and out of reach for many of its citizens. The arrival of COVID-19 has further exposed our system's vulnerability. Despite our best individual and collective intentions, we continue to struggle because of a myopic approach to strategy and a lack of the right people at the planning table. Where are the physicians, nurses, pharmacists, therapists, and   psychologists? And what about the patients?

We must take bold action to improve our current unimpressive healthcare score card. In his book *Rebuilding Trust in Healthcare*, Dr. Paul Pender goes to the "operating room" to dissect the problems of the ailing American healthcare system. He takes a holistic approach to methodically identify the individual components of our complex healthcare machine and then provides comprehensive and attainable solutions.

The genius of this book resides in the basic premise that the patient is at the center of the healthcare universe and that no true progress can be made without a fundamental, unbreakable trust between a patient and a physician. That can be accomplished only if physicians, not bureaucrats or insurance companies, call the shots in the exam room and beyond. *Rebuilding Trust* offers an opportunity for us to reflect on the true ills of the American healthcare system and how to repair it."

–Tomasz Jankowski, DPT, MHA, MBA

"Dr. Pender has written an important and timely book. With the Covid-19 pandemic, Americans find themselves at a crossroads. We have been led to believe that having health insurance equals access to quality healthcare. Proponents of Medicare for all (single payer) now want us to believe that the government is the answer, but doubling down on the most expensive aspects of the healthcare system allowing the government to be the final arbiter on what constitutes healthcare is not the answer. It lies in the trust engrained in the doctor and patient relationship. The doctor as an advocate and the patient as a healthcare consumer is the way to heal our healthcare system by transferring the power back to those for whom the healthcare system is supposed to work. Dr. Pender's prescription for a post-pandemic America is a must read."

–Elaina George, MD, author of Big Medicine: The Cost of Corporate Control and How Doctors and Patients Working Together Can Rebuild a Better System

This book is dedicated to my patients, who have placed their trust in me for their medical and surgical eye care and have inspired me in so many ways.

"We are quite literally drowning in data and a story helps us find a signal through the noise."

From *Unraveling Insanity and Other Stories: Narratives of a Forensic Psychiatrist*, by Albert Drukteinis, MD, JD

Table of Contents

Acknowledgments

I COULDN'T HAVE WRITTEN THIS BOOK without the help of Susan Aiello, DVM, ELS, an experienced editor and writing coach. She mentored me to develop better writing skills. Nancy Cleary deserves special thanks for helping me navigate the process of book publication.

I extend my sincere appreciation to my patients for the trust they placed in me over a professional career spanning four decades. To my mentors and colleagues in medicine, thank you for your guidance and example of professionalism. And to my wife, Joanne, I thank you for your love and support, and for understanding my need for action in the face of challenges.

Advocating for patients is something we should be doing as physicians. Working with the principals of Vxtra Health has helped me to imagine a pathway for better healthcare, and I am grateful to Larry Hightower and his team for including me in their journey.

– Paul Pender, MD

Foreword

PAUL PENDER, MD, HAS WRITTEN a timely, current and thoughtful narrative on a topic of vital importance to all. The issues addressed have been building for years and have become even more urgent and obvious during the recent COVID-19 pandemic. Dr. Pender writes in a direct style and communicates personally with the reader. You feel his concern for patients and, as he notes: "We are all patients." He outlines a problem that is basic to healthcare, in a logical, stepwise narrative, with many examples from his personal experience during his lengthy career as a practicing ophthalmologist. This story is happening now, and it is as real as the virus that has changed the world.

Dr. Pender crafted this book following the time-honored medical system known as the clinical method. The chapters are named after each step in the process whereby a physician puts together the patient's complaints, symptoms, past history, and examination findings, and then formulates a diagnosis and treatment plan. The patient in this tale is the healthcare system, and Dr. Pender is the doctor. Dr. Pender's thesis develops with examples and current references from books, interviews and other sources. He presents his findings and the causes of the problem with trust in the current healthcare system. His solutions, or treatment recommendations, are revealed in the final chapter, after he conducts a lively "ZOOM" meeting with presentations by fictional composite experts from all sides of the healthcare landscape. His clever use of this contemporary virtual meeting platform provides an effective way to explain and summarize the multifaceted nature of the problem. His solution provides hope for restoring trust.

It is not surprising that Dr. Pender could, and did, write this story. He always was, and remains, a good observer of his profession, and he has never been shy about doing something to improve it. He had a long, productive and successful career as a practicing ophthalmologist, keeping up-to-date with the latest techniques, research and teaching during his clinical years. Outside of direct patient care, Dr. Pender was very active in both the national and New England ophthalmology professional world. He gave of his time and provided leadership to these societies. He was on the Board of the New England Ophthalmological Society for many years, an organization of 700 ophthalmologists from all six New England states, serving as Treasurer and then President. He was bestowed a rare honor by that society—a biennial lecture in his name, given by experts in cataract and refractive surgery. *Rebuilding Trust* is the latest example of Paul's continuing contributions and dedication to the medical profession.

– Michael Bradbury, MD
Executive Director
New England Ophthalmological Society

Introduction

THE CORONAVIRUS PANDEMIC that began sweeping the world in late 2019 may have robbed us of many lives and our livelihood, but not of our hope. We have been inspired by the courage and determination of first responders in over 180 countries afflicted by COVID-19. We have admired the persistence of patients in their will to recover despite the attack of the virus and its uncertain prognosis. Fear of the unknown can be mitigated in part by the pursuit of reliable treatments. As of this writing, treatments that prove to work consistently against the coronavirus are elusive. However, we reach out for any signals that may show the way toward conquering this invisible enemy. We have placed our trust in medical professionals who have the expertise to limit its spread and to predict the outcome of the pandemic. This scourge has shocked our collective consciousness, and we wonder, as survivors, what is to become of our scorched earth.

We haven't experienced a pandemic like this in over a hundred years, and it's turned our world upside down. Congress has passed, and the President has signed into law, measures designed to help families and businesses recover from the damage to our health and to our economy. How we respond to this crisis will say a lot about our character, ingenuity and resilience. Hopefully, our response will also point the way to improvements, both in delivering healthcare and in bolstering the patient-physician relationship that has been undermined by internal and external factors.

Perhaps the pause we're taking through our current physical distancing measures will allow us to envision ways to prepare for any future assaults by infectious agents. Caught unprepared by the scale and intensity of this viral epidemic, we may eventually steel ourselves with a greater abundance of protective equipment and with treatments for both acute and asymptomatic cases. The pandemic serves as a wake-up call for a conversation about improvements needed in healthcare and its delivery.

To make a recommendation for restoring trust in healthcare is to invite the charge of hubris when addressing so complex an issue. However, that is my mission. One way to approach this mission is to imagine presenting an unknown case to a panel of medical experts. The traditional approach to such a presentation is well known to the medical community. A glance at the table of contents offers an outline of the thesis that drives this narrative. Starting with a chief complaint, the presenter essentially gives the symptom or the main reason why the patient came in for that visit. In this case, the chief complaint is distrust in healthcare. The history of present illness describes the chief complaint, distrust, in greater detail and within the context of the broader issue of its impact on the patient-physician relationship and the healthcare delivery system. Items to be presented to the expert panel include pertinent symptoms (and an exclusion of others not pertinent). The topics of past history, medications used, allergies, social history, and family history round out the analysis of how distrust in healthcare has evolved. Next, a review of systems that impacts the present illness of distrust must be clarified to establish proper context for the chief complaint. I will argue that trust has been compromised between patients and physicians long before COVID-19 hit, leading to serious disruptions for both those who receive care and those who provide it. The physical exam of our hypothetical case alerts the panel of experts to further clues as to how trust has been compromised. Diagnostic tests are then ordered to help narrow the search for causes, including an analysis of the failure of healthcare systems to meet their intended goals. Finally, the assessment of the problems created by distrust, and the plans for their correction, help to formulate the prescription for rebuilding trust. Such plans derive their strength from a patient-centered model for healthcare delivery.

When a doctor chooses a prescription for a patient, the decision is based on known facts of the indications, contraindications, actions, and potential side effects of that treatment across a broad portion of the population. We can't predict with certainty how an individual patient will respond, but we believe that the treatment will take care of the problem. I can't claim omniscience for how we go about rebuilding trust in healthcare, but I can offer my perspective with the hope that it will have a positive effect.

I consider the relationship between the individual patient and physician a sacred pact—an expression of mutual trust dating back to the time of the ancient Greeks. When I became a physician, I took the Hippocratic oath, an expression of altruism toward my fellow human beings. However, working in the world of modern medical care, doctors face challenges for living up to the tenets of the oath. Furthermore, as physicians, we must address serious problems created in an adversarial healthcare system.

These challenges become the focus of this book on rebuilding trust in healthcare. Above all, we must ensure that the best interests of the patient are honored, represented faithfully and delivered with integrity. Only then can we create a better healthcare system for America.

Advocating for patients and for physicians has been a passion of mine throughout a medical career spanning four decades. Once I retired from private practice in ophthalmology, I took to online forums for my advocacy as part of my strategy to develop better writing skills. It was through such writing that I was invited to advise a healthcare company looking to launch a new model of patient-centered care, led by doctors and their teams of distinction as the driving force for reform. As part of my prescription for rebuilding trust in healthcare, I will discuss in detail how this model would apply to solving the myriad problems we now face.

It is my view that the patient-doctor relationship should serve as the fundamental building block for any proposal to fix our healthcare system. That relationship should not be an afterthought by insurance companies or by government, designed from top-down to capture "lives" for their subscriber rolls. The current system is not sustainable. My prescription is a roadmap to smarter reform that would begin the process of rebuilding trust in healthcare.

At some point in our lives, we all become patients. Therefore, it is in our best interest to face up to the challenges of developing a more responsive and responsible system of healthcare. Doing so will begin to rebuild the trust we expect and deserve.

Chapter 1

Chief Complaint

WHAT HAPPENED TO OUR TRUST IN HEALTHCARE? You may
have asked yourself that question a lot lately. The coronavirus pandemic has placed our healthcare vulnerabilities
front and center. Distrust about the origin and virulence
of coronavirus and the supply chain charged with meeting
its challenge has underscored concerns that have been
smoldering for some time. We have felt overwhelmed by a
wave of uncertainty hitting our healthcare system like a
tsunami. We ask ourselves, what sources propagated that
wave in the first place? Distrust in our healthcare has
impacted both those receiving it and those providing it.

Our dependence on a viable healthcare system and its
providers has come to occupy an uncomfortable place in
our minds, especially in a time of crisis. This book will
examine sources for distrust in healthcare and recommend
a path toward rebuilding that trust. While the fundamental
building block for restoring confidence in our system of
healthcare arises first from the relationship forged between
patients and their doctors, our leaders in multiple areas—
insurance, pharmaceuticals, government, public health—
must share in the mission with skill, compassion and
integrity. That's a lot to ask, but as Americans, we have
the power to shape our future.

Before I launch into my story, first a word about our
calling as doctors and fellow healthcare workers. We don't
practice in a digital vacuum, yet we are charged with more

frequent and more detailed documentation of our encounters with patients. Lately, it hasn't been a pretty picture.

Recapturing Our Humanity as Doctors[1]

So much of what I read from the futurists is the stuff of science fiction without the humanity. We now have cellphones with facial recognition for identification (and to create effective and personal emojis). Artificial intelligence is being developed to gauge the emotional state associated with facial expressions, something physicians have developed over years of clinical practice. Unfortunately, that ability to look a patient in the eye, to discern if the entire story is being shared or only a synopsis of the problem, is compromised by the doctor turning to check boxes on the computer.

If there is a universal complaint I have heard from patients who see harried primary care physicians (PCPs), it is the feeling of being disconnected from their care provider. There may be multiple causes for this assessment, but the one most often cited by patients and by doctors alike is the documentation requirement imposed upon the medical profession. There is little face-to-face time allotted for the visit, and often the patient's face is pointed toward the physician's back. Hospitalists are charged with treating sick individuals they may have never seen before, sometimes managing data without doing a thorough physical exam. Since the vast majority of primary care practices are now owned by hospitals or large clinics, financial pressures require that outpatient care be the exclusive domain of the primary care physician while unscheduled urgent conditions be shunted to hospital-affiliated urgent care centers.

The PCP, the physician best equipped to know the emotional and physical needs of the inpatient, is not only discouraged from making hospital rounds but is barred from writing orders or performing procedures that are part of a PCP's skill set. Humanity and pride of purpose for physicians are sacrificed for efficiency and the demands of payers.

If artificial means are designed to recognize patterns to predict illness and guide our care of patients, physicians must ensure that our patients trust us to perform properly as healers, not merely as mechanics working on a complex machine. That trust can be eroded by dependence on technology to give us answers, when in fact we need more as human beings. Physicians are taught, first, to do no harm to our patients. But understanding patients' emotional needs is also critical. Skill without compassion is not a formula for success, nor is it what patients deserve.

Working with a scribe for the last five years of my medical career allowed me to engage with my patients without having to endlessly toil over a computer. Scribes should be discreet during patient encounters so that patients can freely discuss personal details in confidence, face to face, while the medical record is documented in the background. I dictated findings to my scribe, and then translated the jargon "into plain English" for the patient after the exam was completed. I asked if there were any questions, and made sure to answer them before I left the room. The patient then checked out with printed instructions and a recommendation for a return appointment in hand. Letters to referring doctors and primary care physicians were created on the spot. I may have glanced at the visit note before

I signed off to ensure that the diagnostic and procedure codes were accurate, but I didn't take work home to complete documentation, as some physicians do. Working with a scribe allowed me to practice ophthalmology the way I was trained. Reading body language is part of that skill set for me, something I would not replace with a machine.

Having good rapport with patients is critical for determining underlying causes that adversely affect their health. Showing that we care as physicians is essential to establishing that rapport. After all, patients are checking out our body language as well.

This book will tell a complex story of what is needed for trust to develop and how it became compromised. It will describe where we are now, in the middle of a pandemic, trying to assess the physical and psychological damage to our healthcare workers, as well as the economic damage to facilities and practices. And finally, I will assess the problems diagnosed and will suggest possible treatment plans that may positively impact the future of healthcare and how it is delivered. Rebuilding trust won't be easy, but it's vital to our responsibilities for the health of all Americans.

Chapter 2

History of Present Illness

A PATIENT DEVELOPS TRUST from a perception that doctors care, even as medical students with few skills. In the course of medical training, some doctors responsible for teaching medical students consider them merely as observers to the process of interacting with patients. "These can be important student–doctor learning experiences, but they do not qualify as authentic, engaged health care roles because students are 'educational bystanders' in care delivery processes."[2] Such comments invite criticism of the arrogance of the speaker. Even as students, we can help patients to alleviate their fear of the unknown. An example of gaining trust from a desperate patient occurred during my first clinical rotation on internal medicine as a third-year student.

1001 Arabian Nights

A late admission arrived on the ward where I was assigned. Many beds were lined up against the walls with only curtains to draw for privacy. There were no sinks at the bedside for hand washing. The conditions for both doctors and patients were primitive in many ways back in the 1970s.

I was directed to a middle-aged woman sitting on the edge of her bed, jaundiced, confused and anxious. Wearing only a hospital johnny, she appeared very sick to me. I observed the Chief Resident as he conducted a mental

9

status exam on the patient, trying to assess her level of orientation to person, place and time. Person was OK, time was irrelevant, and place was a non-starter.

"Ms. Adams, can you please name three states in the United States?" the Chief Resident asked.

"Alaska, Nebraska..." the patient paused, trying to think of another answer.

"What state are you in now?"

"A state of confusion!" Ms. Adams yelled with a Brooklyn accent, and we couldn't help but laugh. She had no history of drug or alcohol abuse, no history of liver or gallbladder disease. Her only surgical history was a breast tumor with extension to regional lymph nodes treated by lumpectomy several years ago. The residents in charge of her care viewed Ms. Adams as a diagnostic mystery, one they were determined to solve. To help minimize her anxiety, I was assigned to hold her hand during the many tests that she underwent. We became friends in the process, so much so that she made the analogy of our pre-test banter to that of Scheherazade of *1001 Arabian Nights*. I did my best to entertain her while she waited for the liver scan that would shed light on the cause of her jaundice and depressed mental status. Metastatic breast cancer that targeted her liver and the bile duct was the root of her symptoms. Her mental status gradually improved with treatment, and she was discharged after a course of chemotherapy to the care of her local oncologist.

A month later, I was summoned to the ward clerk's station to see a visitor. Ms. Adams returned to thank me for my kindness and support during her hospitalization. She wore bright red lipstick and a big smile as she presented me with the orchestral version of Rimsky-Korsakov's *1001 Arabian Nights*. I was touched that she would present me with a gift. I didn't solve her medical mystery, far from it. But I did help her, emotionally and psychologically, get through a tough patch while in the hospital, and she was grateful. I later learned, within a month of her unannounced visit to see me, she had succumbed to the cancer.

Ms. Adams first presented with confusion, a symptom associated with the toxic effects of high bilirubin in her bloodstream. The bilirubin was also causing the jaundice, including a yellowing of the whites of her eyes. She had several medical issues, but the biggest factor I had to deal with as a student was her fear. She had no local family or friends. Her thinking was clouded, and she was alone in the hospital, in unfamiliar surroundings. She expressed her fear openly, and the doctors assigned to her care were less committed to dealing with her emotional state than to determining the cause of her physical symptoms. By talking her off the ledge, I connected with her in a very human way, helping to ease her fear of the unknown. I have put that principle to work in my practice of ophthalmology, the specialty of medical and surgical care of patients with problems relating to their eyes.

Often, the body language and facial expression of a patient tell a great deal about the fear associated with a condition that can potentially compromise one of our most important senses—our ability to see. By explaining the nature of the problem using a large desktop plastic model of the eye, I put into simple language what the patient needs to know about the condition and what I propose to do about it.

A woman recently returned to see me about cataracts I'd diagnosed a month earlier. At her prior visit, she expressed fear that, after the surgery, she wouldn't be able to lift her 150-pound brother with Down syndrome, for whom she was the primary caregiver. She assumed that there would be restrictions for lifting in the immediate post-op period. Her primary objection to going ahead with the procedure was not about the surgery itself but about the aftercare. She put off the decision, knowing that she needed to see better (intellectually) but unable to accept the notion of her eyeball being cut (emotionally). She categorized the two components of decision-making, intellectual and emotional, as equally necessary, and I concurred. She asked to discuss with me the risks and benefits of cataract surgery, the options for the type of intraocular lens that would be inserted, and the needed post-op care, including any medication and other concerns such as restrictions on lifting. Thankfully, she didn't require 1001 nights to reach her decision, and her surgery went well.

I present these examples of gaining trust through empathy to demonstrate patients' needs for support in the face of the unknown. Fear of the unknown, whether from loss of sight or from the threat of COVID-19, creates anxiety. Physicians are not simply body mechanics working to solve a puzzle or replace a part. They can and should offer hope and comfort as they apply knowledge to find a solution. But most of all, patients should have a reason to trust physicians to care for their needs. Patients need to know that physicians are in their corner for whatever the fight may be.

Medical education has vastly improved since I graduated from medical school in the mid-1970s. Currently, there are more opportunities to engage patients early in the educational process during the basic science years of study. For medical students who don't want to become clinicians, numerous opportunities are available for research. Lab work has proved vitally important in the study of the coronavirus, and medical researchers have brought their studies to public view that may have lived only in obscure medical journals before the pandemic. We are grateful for the signals coming from private companies and from publicly funded laboratories about potential treatments, especially those that act to temper the exaggerated immune response of the host[3] and those that attempt to kill the virus.[4] A recent poll[5] of over a thousand US adults asked the question:

"Regardless of how often you get information from these sources, how much do you trust information provided about the coronavirus outbreak by each of the following?"

Not surprisingly, two-thirds of respondents trusted the Centers for Disease Control and healthcare providers a great deal or quite a bit, 25% a moderate amount, and single digits for little trust or none at all. Contrast that level of public trust in social media at 11% as quite a bit, 26% a moderate amount, and 63% little or none at all. I will have more to say in a section on the impact of social media on the public's trust in healthcare. But for now, let's stick with the subject of doctors of medicine and osteopathy, MDs and DOs.

The study of medicine assumes that you will become a life-long learner. Doctors in New Hampshire, and in most every state in the US, are required to maintain their license to practice by taking 100 hours of credits of continuing medical education (CME) every two years that meet the high standards for current study established by the Accreditation Council for Continuing Medical Education. Educating physicians already licensed has become a thriving business. The specialty boards now require maintenance of certification in most specialties of medicine, a controversial topic to say the least. Once board certified in a specialty, physicians must not only maintain their license through CME courses, but also must study for another exam and pay thousands of dollars for the privilege of being board certified once again (for a period of several years, and then the process must be repeated). The maintenance of certification designation has been used to determine renewal of hospital privileges, so the pressure never really goes away to take study courses and to pass exams. Doctors ask, "Where is the trust that was conferred upon successful completion of my original board certification? Are my 100 hours of CME credit every two years meaningless for the specialty board?" The argument for supporting the recertification process stems mainly from a perceived need for policing of doctors, by doctors. The argument goes, "if we don't take responsibility for ensuring the competence of our peers, someone else will do it for us." I would expect that in the immediate future, the issue will not be resolved to the satisfaction of all clinicians, and the resentment for lack of trust from the medical establishment will persist.

Some institutions of higher learning have developed programs for medical professionals who are managers in healthcare, serving as administrators and chiefs of medical services in large clinics and hospitals. These programs are not cheap. The following course description is taken from the registration form for a 6-day conference put on by the Harvard Macy Institute[6]:

"The Harvard Macy Institute's A Systems Approach to Assessment in Health Professions Education is designed to encourage participants to apply systems thinking in designing assessment programs to support the continuous quality improvement of students/trainees, faculty, and curricula at their academic health science institutions. The program incorporates multiple pedagogical methods, including interactive presentations, case discussions, small group journal clubs, institutional planning groups, electives (focused mini-sessions/workshops on assessment tools and approaches), and consultations with faculty experts. During this intensive 6-day program, educators and administrators from diverse health science disciplines will be introduced to key concepts from system theory, best practices in educational assessment, and mini-workshops focused on specific assessment approaches. Throughout the program, participants will also have an opportunity to apply systems principles in case discussions depicting problematic assessment situations and to plan an assessment/evaluation design to implement at their home institution."

The fee of $4500 does not include hotel stay and meals, and it does not count the lost revenue from clinical practice over the 6 days of the course. Admittedly, it is expensive. The question is whether or not the course is well designed for its target audience. I question the "systems" approach and the catch phrases about "continuous quality improvement." They remind me of what factory managers must deal with on a production line. If there are gaps in our healthcare delivery system, we should begin improvements by focusing on the trust we are attempting to create with our patients, and then design a system around those elements. There is much more to come on this subject in later sections, so please remain patient.

When we think about the trust patients put in physicians, there are certain assumptions to be made. The first and foremost assumption is that physicians are looking out for the best interests of their patients, regardless of their source of income. Fee-for-service medicine, representing the exchange of money for the service rendered between two parties, is rapidly becoming extinct. Third parties (commercial insurance companies, the federal government and others) determine what can be covered and what can be reimbursed as "medically necessary." Second, the healthcare system that employs physicians is an important consideration for some patients, that is, whether the physician works on salary for a large hospital system or clinic. The assumption here is that physicians have no incentive to order more tests or to pad their bill for unnecessary services, because those measures don't add to the physician's personal bottom line. I'll probe deeper into the topic of economic incentives in later sections, but on the surface, the idea seems legitimate. Let's look at some notions of trust derived from popular journalism and from scholarly articles.

Some reporters in the media have referred to countries as "low-trust" (America) and "high-trust" (European model) depending on their level of nationalized healthcare.[7] The response to the coronavirus epidemic shows a dichotomy between two forms of healthcare delivery. According to these models, a high-trust country has a broader safety net for the less fortunate and a population more willing to follow orders. Sweden, a high-trust country, has urged its populace to use reasonable measures like social distancing and to protect its most vulnerable groups but has not applied draconian measures to shut down its economy. In contrast, New York City, as the epicenter of the coronavirus pandemic in the United States[8], reflects a low-trust environment with greater numbers of people requiring assistance and individuals less accepting of strict measures imposed by the governor. More time is needed to determine the ultimate outcomes for both Sweden and New York City, but the question of trusting the public to do the right thing remains controversial. Some academics claim that patients favor their interactions within a nationalized healthcare system to one that is "co-modified," that is, a system of many parts. Yet the level of trust for doctors in either system remains high regardless of the healthcare system studied.[9] Compassion motivates doctors and their staffs; this is more important to patients than the system in which health professionals work.

The healthcare system and employment structure, however, can have adverse effects on doctors and their attitudes. I will cover this concept in greater detail in the chapter on Review of Systems. You are well aware of the impact of stress on frontline healthcare professionals fighting COVID-19. But the reality is that an unfolding of the fears and concerns faced by doctors have preceded the attack of the virus. The issue of "burnout" among physicians has garnered attention long before the epidemic caused by the coronavirus. Patients may begin to distrust their doctor, fearing that they are receiving inadequate attention from a health provider who seems mentally uncommitted to the job. The following findings are noted in a recent medical journal article[10]:

"Burnout in physicians is characterized by emotional exhaustion, finding work no longer meaningful, feelings of ineffectiveness, and a tendency to view patients, students, and colleagues as objects rather than as human beings. Associated manifestations include headache, insomnia, tension, anger, narrow-mindedness, impaired memory, decreased attention, and thoughts of quitting. In certain situations, physical exhaustion and moral distress are prominent features."

The paper goes into greater detail of the causes, consequences and possible cures of physician burnout. I have described the adverse effects our healthcare system is having on its doctors.[11]

Burdens and Burnout

Writing and speaking about the changes in healthcare that have occurred in the last few decades have spawned a cottage industry online. On the social media website for physicians founded by Kevin Pho, MD, we learn about what issues concern doctors, nurses and patients. The exchanges posted seem to foster a sense of group therapy—and for good cause. There is a lot of angst among physicians about their roles in this ever-changing healthcare landscape. Perhaps the most serious problem deals with the negative effects of increasing administrative burdens every practicing physician must face.

With his usual keen insight, in a series of two syndicated columns for *The Washington Post* in June 2015, Charles Krauthammer, MD, attempted to identify the reasons *Why Doctors Quit*.[12] Although the columnist had not practiced psychiatry since finishing his medical training, he had observed how physicians felt the damaging effects of responsibility without autonomy. Responsibility for the care of patients, without commensurate autonomy to make medical decisions in the patient's best interest, induces feelings of a lack of self-worth.

Today, physicians face many hurdles in doing what is right for their patients. Obtaining preauthorization for simple tests and lab work frustrates the physician and creates an atmosphere of constantly being kept "on hold" while waiting for permission to move forward with medically necessary orders. "Step-therapy," defined here as progressively administering drugs or treatments if the simplest measures prove unsuccessful, may cause actual harm if a more complex (read expensive) treatment should have been chosen in the first place. Such decisions for care, micromanaged by the federal government and payers, remove the physician's autonomy to make appropriate medical decisions. Then there is the burden of documentation, the filling out of computer codes denoting the level of all work done and every decision made. No longer is it considered acceptable to handwrite notes in the patient's chart. In fact, unless medical records and claims are maintained and filed electronically, the doctor's practice is fined by payers for noncompliance. A lot of doctors feel cornered, boxed in by their desire to continue serving their patients, yet unable to lighten the administrative burdens of modern medical practice.

Reports from physician surveys conducted nationwide paint a bleak picture of the mindset of doctors. In a 2019 Medscape poll of 15,000 physicians, from family doctors to surgeons of all stripes, nearly half the respondents reported symptoms of burnout, defined as feelings of job dissatisfaction with elements of hopelessness. One in seven respondents, according to the survey and sensationalized in the *New York Post*, have considered suicide. These findings should, indeed, raise alarms. The Band-Aid approach has been to foster "mindfulness," to increase exercise to promote endorphin release and to open up channels of communication among peers. However, these superficial measures remind me of the fable of the boy sticking his finger in the dike to prevent the flood. The boy stayed there all night, in spite of the cold, until the adults of the village find him and make the necessary repairs. But where are the necessary repairs for disaffected physicians?

While some physician counselors talk about relieving doctors of the demands imposed by documentation requirements, there is little action on the part of US Health and Human Services to lessen the burden. In fact, the entire fabric of reimbursement for physician services is made up of bullet points and quality measures that don't really address quality. Too much emphasis has been placed on process rather than on outcomes. Further complicating the formula for physician payment is the notion that somehow federal government officials can determine accurately how exhaustive a doctor's use of resources costs the system.

How an individual doctor's decisions cost the system are being used for "economic credentialing" by hospitals in attempts to "eliminate waste." For surgeons, their graded "success" and reimbursement depend on hitting targets, such as the number of eyes in which a cataract surgeon achieves 20/40 or better vision (the eyesight needed to drive a car), divided by the total number of cataract surgeries performed. It is simply naive to believe that a higher score for patient comorbidities, like glaucoma or macular degeneration, can be factored into worse outcomes for cataract surgery without creating disincentives for doctors to tackle patients with multiple medical problems. If reimbursement depends on the best possible outcomes, why would a surgeon take on patients who have a higher risk of complications? Under the current system, it is easier, and more lucrative, to simply refer those patients elsewhere. And what does that imply for referral centers, such as academic institutions? They will get the most complicated, sickest patients, shipped out of their local communities.

Part of the symptom complex of burnout for doctors includes feelings of helplessness in a profession designed to help. When it seems like physicians are stymied in doing what they do best—that is, taking care of patients—either because of time constraints or administrative demands, doctors begin to question why they stay in the field. They wonder if all the sacrifices of time and sleep and the hundreds of hours of training have really been worth it. Pride of purpose is eroded by the grind of the insignificant, and doctors feel like they are drowning in a sea of minutia dictated by outside forces.

For doctors, according to the surveys, the satisfaction derived from patient care is still the prime motivator to entering and staying in medicine. Finding ways to enhance physician satisfaction while minimizing frustrations is a challenge. For doctors to recapture their humanity, they must be able to focus on the patient and to reduce or eliminate burnout through delegation of clerical tasks. Or perhaps, like me, doctors could retire from practicing medicine and write about the changes to come.

The mindset of my fellow professionals concerns me as a physician. And it should concern you as well if you are reading this book. From my perspective as a physician, the direction in which we go as a society depends in large part on the integrity and competence of its healthcare workforce. I feel strongly about the need to support the people who look out for us as patients.[13]

A Physician Writes for Catharsis

After finishing my pitch for my book, *Making Lives Better: How Mentors and Patients Inspired a Doctor's Work* at the Harvard Writers' Conference in Boston, I felt relieved and encouraged by the judges' comments. As I waited for my turn at the podium, I glanced above my notes over the faces of 300 of my fellow attendees who had accomplished so much in their respective fields of medicine, nursing and counseling. The pitches made by these wound-be authors revealed an amazing resilience to the human condition. One attendee had been put up for adoption and became a prostitute in order to survive his surroundings. Another speaker, a physician father, reported his son's road to 'recovery' from heroin addiction, captured in his late son's journal. The doctor proposed ways for parents to intervene before it is too late. The meeting erupted in applause when he finished his pitch. Women described ways for becoming 'badass' to face discrimination and attempted sexual harassment. How to overcome psychological and physical wounds became a recurrent theme. The challenge for many of those pitching an idea for a book in 70 seconds or less involved relating individual stories of triumph over tragedy. Often, the presenters exposed themselves to an emotional cauldron to bare their hearts and souls to fellow attendees.

Pitch coaches labored unselfishly to strengthen what we proposed to write without a hint of condescension. These committed professionals led us on a journey of creation, improvement and commitment. They gave us confidence in our work and mission. If we don't believe in our work, who will? The course organizer, Julie Silver, MD, created a supportive environment for stretching our talents and for surrendering control to the experts.

The energy level of attendees was unlike anything I have experienced. Dr. Silver assembled a dynamic faculty and scheduled time for interaction with publishers and agents. Returning for a second helping of how to write non-fiction in 2019 gave me a greater appreciation of what I want to accomplish and the confidence to try something I have not attempted during my medical career.

I remain hopeful that the patient stories that inspired me in practice may be shared with a larger audience.

In order to further inspire my writing efforts, one of my coaches referred me to a physician-writer known for his remarkable prose. His TED talks have been viewed online by thousands of people. Abraham Verghese, MD, describes his approach to writing as follows.[14]

"I celebrate such writing and the impulse to write, the impulse to share some transformative incident that I am privileged to have witnessed. In my own writing, I often feel that I write in order to understand what I am thinking. Mysteriously, insight comes (when it does come) in the very act of writing as if only by sitting with pen and pad can we snatch it out of the ether."

What sets his writing apart is Verghese's way of seeing healthcare challenges through the eyes of the patient. From his TED biography, we learn that he spent a year as a hospital orderly, working at the bottom of the medical education pecking order, to better understand the person behind the illness. That experience has shaped his development as a doctor and a writer. He founded the Center for Medical Humanities & Ethics at the University of Texas and later joined the Stanford medical faculty as a Professor for the Theory and Practice of Medicine. Dr. Verghese is my role model for a doctor and a medical writer. *The New York Times* offered the following observation[15].

"Art and medicine may seem disparate worlds, but Dr. Verghese insists that for him they are one. Doctors and writers are both collectors of stories."

The stories of patients I have acquired in the four decades of medical practice are compelling. They have informed my thinking and my writing. They have helped shape the doctor I am, and the writer I want to be. For me, the key ingredient in the formula for a robust patient-doctor relationship is trust. What follows is a story from my work as an eye surgeon.

A History Lesson

The wiry, talkative professor, accustomed to giving assignments and directions in her college courses, was now on the receiving end. An avid reader and outdoors person, her cataracts were getting in the way of her lifestyle, and she was going to need my help. After a lengthy discussion of her surgical options, she decided that great distance vision without glasses was a priority following surgery. Right upfront, she said that she expected me to meet the highest standards of surgical care. She appraised me like she might regard a student of some promise, but one who needed to be made aware of her expectations. Professor G had approached retirement from the university as another of life's adventures, welcoming the chance to kayak on the ocean and to hike in the mountains. She was frustrated that her poor vision held her back, and she was going to do something about it. Life wasn't worth living if one couldn't see, according to this college professor of history. She watched the consent video on cataract and lens implant surgery, received answers to her questions, signed the permit and booked her case with the surgical coordinator. That was that.

On the day of surgery as part of the pre-surgical exam, I listen to the heart and lungs of every patient. As I approached Professor G, I warmed the head of the stethoscope in the palm of my hand to avoid shocking her with a cold instrument. As I pressed my stethoscope to the johnny over her chest, I heard a soft, crunching sound. I looked under the garment for the source of her muffled heart sounds.

What I saw shocked me! The professor had taped a laminated sheet of paper to her chest, a legal document stating DO NOT RESUSCITATE in the case of cardiac arrest!

"You really expect me to honor your request not to try and save you if there is a problem?" I couldn't believe what I read on the document, single-spaced and covering her entire torso.

"I've had a good life so far, and I live alone. If I don't make it, who cares?"

"Well, I care. You saw the sign as you entered the Surgicenter. We will use appropriate measures in the event of a major problem. If you want me to remove your cataract, we need to monitor your heart, and this document is in the way. Just how am I to apply the electrodes to your chest with your DNR sign in place?" I suppressed a laugh as I shook my head.

"OK, then. I'll remove the sign. But you know how I feel about extraordinary measures." The professor gave me a serious look with furrowed eyebrows.

"I understand. I'll do whatever it takes to make your surgery successful. Now let's proceed, shall we?" I helped her remove the sign. Her heartbeat sounded strong, with a regular rate and rhythm. She had refused any sedation pre-op, wanting to be fully aware of her surroundings and my commands while undergoing surgery under topical anesthesia only. Fortunately, her surgery went flawlessly, and the next day she saw 20/20 at distance without eyeglasses.

"When can you do the other eye, doctor?" the professor asked.

"If all goes well, and you use your eye drops as directed, we can plan to do the other eye in a couple of weeks." I sensed that she would follow her post-op instructions carefully.

"Very well. Thank you for your fine care, doctor," she said as she shook my hand and left the exam room.

I came to admire Professor G as I learned more about her life. She had received little encouragement at home. As a child, her strict father told her that he didn't expect much from her in school. He was surprised by her academic success. She made it a point to achieve all that she could in her studies, reaching the level of full professor and serving as an example to women in the university setting. "You always have to prove your worth," she was fond of saying.

I enjoyed taking care of Professor G. She felt the need to broaden my education, offering me lists of must-read books. The history books she adored included those written by Dean Acheson, former US Secretary of State, and George Marshall, former Secretary of State and Defense, whose Marshall Plan rebuilt Europe after the end of World War II. Professor G wouldn't leave the exam chair until she impressed upon me, time and again, that to be well read meant to read and to understand history.

The professor wrote me a short letter the evening of her first eye surgery. Her letterhead showed six owls with various expressions and captions, including decaf (tired look), half-caf (one-and-a-half eyes open), regular (both eyes open), Irish coffee (both eyes half-open, smiling), espresso (wide eyes), and double espresso (very wide eyes).

I quote from her letter:

"Dear Doctor Pender,

...picked up your gracious call of concern at 5 pm: All is well, weller and wellest—indeed. All (sensations) gone, both reading and distance. Vision sharp as a tack.

The-"regular-citation" that I forgot yesterday: A FAR-THER SHORE; THE LIFE AND LEGACY OF RACHEL CARSON, William Souder. Carson, one of the three most significant women of the 20th century. She, mother of conservation and preservation. Margaret Sanger, who let women out of a Prison, and Eleanor Roosevelt, First Lady of the World, as said Winston Churchill. All three indispensable.

Most cordial thanks, Professor G."

I kept the lists of must-read books. I have accumulated many recommendations from the professor over the years, and with my own retirement approaching, I hope to read some of them. I just wish I had had her for my professor when I was in college.

Trust must be earned, and hard-earned trust can begin to erode from misunderstandings. Problems arise when patients do not understand which services are covered under their health plan and which are not. Part of the skepticism patients experience with billings from their doctors comes from the enclosed "Explanation of Benefits." Patients are unaware that some medical services are deemed either "not medically necessary" or are not included in coverage determinations. A typical example of a misunderstanding of Medicare Advantage coverage has to do with eye care. While such plans tout eye exams and glasses benefits not included in regular Medicare programs, these actual benefits hardly live up to their advertisements. For example, diabetic patients should have a complete medical eye exam to look for damage to the blood vessels in the back of the eye every year. Such an exam is considered part of best medical practices, but the "eye exam" allowed by Medicare Advantage to which the patient is entitled without a co-pay falls well below the standard for a complete medical eye exam. The patient discovers that the Medicare Advantage benefit only covers a cursory exam, including refraction, a determination of the need for corrective lenses not covered under traditional Medicare. The misunderstanding, derived from the patients' expectations and what doctors are permitted to deliver under their plans, undermines trust in the patient-doctor relationship. When it comes to billing for services rendered, a perceived conflict will quickly damage patients' trust in their doctors and in their healthcare system.[16] No one likes surprises on their bills.

Facing unknown sources of, and consequences from, health problems creates anxiety for patients. Some patients are more demonstrable than others in the way they manifest their worries.

A Patient of Note

"Thank you, doctor. I agree to have eye surgery, but if things don't work out as planned, I'll kill myself." I had no doubt she was serious.

Ms. Proper, a new patient on a busy clinic day, came to see me because she was losing her vision. When I walked into the exam room and introduced myself, she smiled, but with an expression of concern, eyebrows raised, anxious to hear what I would find. Her makeup was exquisitely applied, and she looked much younger than the age indicated by the date of birth listed on her medical record. Elegantly dressed in a burgundy suit and cream blouse, with grey hair styled up to feature pearl earrings and matching necklace, her appearance befitted an evening out more than an appointment with an ophthalmologist.

As I took her history, I learned that she worked full time as an accountant, and her appearance underscored her attention to detail. She had poor vision in one eye since childhood, and she was now losing vision in her only seeing eye due to cataract. Her vision was now so poor that, despite corrective eyeglasses, she was unable to see the diamond ring at the end of her left hand.

"I knew this was coming, doctor."

"The good news is that you have a cataract, a condition we can fix."

"What are my chances for a complete recovery?

"You are a great candidate for surgery. No other medical problems."

She was terrified of losing not only her sight, but also her ability to work and support herself. I went over her options for surgery. She nodded as I explained that the lens of her eye had become cloudy and that it could be replaced with an artificial lens, as well as why I believed she should expect a good outcome for vision postoperatively. Her comment about taking her own life was shocking, but I believed her. Without useful vision, she would lose her job, her driver's license, and her independence.

Ms. Proper was certainly not my first "one-eyed" patient. But in these patients, when only one eye has visual function and the other has limited vision or none at all, the stakes are higher. Surgery becomes the equivalent of a circus high-wire act, without a safety net.

Under normal circumstances, after cataract surgery, patients need to wear an eye patch overnight. In Ms. Proper's case, she would have to spend the night in the hospital, unable to feed herself or to do anything without help. I thought that a different approach might be better for her and started to consider alternatives. While I had done many cataract cases under local anesthesia, unfortunately, that method of numbing the eye would not be the best technique for her, given that I would be operating on her only seeing eye. A local block to the nerves and tissues around the eye would render it useless for most of the day, meaning her only good eye would be covered by an eye patch. There had to be a better way.

I had read about an alternative method of numbing the eye by instilling an anesthetic fluid within the eye, plus eye drops on the outside of the eye (rather than by injecting a liquid anesthetic in the surrounding tissues). This anesthetic technique would eliminate the patient's sensation while preserving vision after surgery, because the optic nerve would not be affected.

I decided to offer Ms. Proper the new method with the understanding that she would have to keep her head very still during surgery. Although she should not feel pain, the anesthetic would not stop eye movement. She wanted to be able to see to do things for herself on the day of her surgery, and she agreed with the plan. And so, she became my first patient to undergo cataract and intraocular lens surgery by topical anesthesia. Ms. Proper received a mild oral sedative an hour before surgery. She needed to be alert enough to follow directions such as looking up into the microscope light and looking down toward her toes, even though her face and body were covered with a sterile drape.

The night before her surgery, I reviewed the concentration of the anesthetic to be instilled within the eye. The next morning, I discussed with the scrub nurse the need for preservative-free lidocaine for injection into the eye. She registered the request with a nod, knowing that this was a first for me. I desperately wanted everything to go well.

In the operating room, I finished Ms. Proper's cataract extraction and lens implantation, and then moved the surgical microscope away from her view. Once the sterile drapes were removed, she looked up and smiled.

"I can see you!"

What a relief, for both patient and surgeon. I called her at home that evening. Her spirits were soaring, watching television with a new meaning for "high definition." I examined Ms. Proper the next morning and recorded vision of 20/20 without eyeglasses for distance. I handed her a pair of reading glasses and a near card with numbers. She read them all.

"When can I go back to work?"

"Tomorrow, if you feel up to it. Wear your reading glasses at the computer and be sure to take your eye drops. I'll see you in a week."

Years later, during a consult at the hospital, a nurse

approached me and said, "Dr. Pender, you did my mother's cataract surgery, and she's very grateful." I looked at the nurse's face and nametag. Neither seemed familiar. Perhaps a married name?

"Please tell me your mother's name."

"Priscilla Proper."

"Oh, yes. I remember her well. She had only one functioning eye, and she told me that if she had a complication from her cataract surgery, she would take her own life."

"Sounds like Mother," she replied.

Can you imagine? Have you ever experienced a statement from your mother that was that over the top? Would you, as the patient, express your fear of losing your vision in a similar way, threatening suicide? If you were the surgeon, attempting a new surgical technique on someone, would you have chosen a different candidate? In retrospect, we all might have done or said something different, but that is life.

When I have retold the story about my first cataract surgery under topical anesthesia to other doctors, their reaction is mixed. "Are you crazy, trying that technique for the first time on someone so emotional?" "You were lucky with the result. You could have had a complication." "Nice job; no fatality." I offered the patient what I believed was in her best interest, the right thing to do. The alternative, hospitalization and a period of total dependence, was unacceptable to her. Since her surgery several years ago, topical anesthesia has become the preferred method for cataract surgery for the right candidate, creating a *"wow"* factor for patients and eye surgeons alike. Achieving great vision after a brief recovery period is now commonplace.

I felt relieved when I completed Ms. Proper's surgery, and I was pleased that she could see well enough to walk out of the operating room with only a clear eye shield for protection. That case stands out in my experience, a patient of note. Her eye surgery impacted all parties concerned, patient, family and surgeon.

As a physician, I have felt privileged to care for my patients and to help them improve and maintain their eyesight. And the great news for the world of ophthalmology is that most patients are happy with their care.

Modern cataract surgery is a product of advanced technology and attention to detail. However, its early proponents had to overcome challenges stemming from manufacturing of lens materials and from a highly skeptical medical establishment. Adding to the challenges were efforts made by activists to obstruct the Food and Drug Administration approvals for these unique pieces of plastic and silicone that would be used to replace the cloudy human lens. Sidney Wolfe, MD, a spokesman for Ralph Nader's Public Citizen group, testified before Congress that the procedure and materials used should be suspended because of surgical complications that he claimed were widespread. To counter his testimony, Robert Young, the late actor who starred as Marcus Welby, MD, in a television series running seven years in the 1970s, gave an impassioned testimony about his own successful cataract and intraocular lens surgery. Before the advent of such advancements, postoperative patients required eyeglasses that were as thick as Coke bottle bottoms. The actor swore that he was able to continue his acting career only because his surgeon had placed the artificial lens inside his eyes to replace the cataract and restore his vision. It was a dramatic moment in the halls of Congress, and progress continued as surgeons reported their results to the FDA on every surgical case for a period of years. Ultimately, the FDA granted approval for the devices.

This story illustrates that doctors who view the Hippocratic oath provision to "first, do no harm" must secure the trust of their patients before introducing a novel treatment. It is vitally important for a discussion to occur about the risks and benefits of the proposed treatment, so that the patient can give informed consent. Patients may file a malpractice suit due to complications that occurred which were not discussed with them before surgery. While doctors are given the benefit of the doubt regarding the extent of the discussion in most cases, juries want to know whether the patient's questions were answered to the patient's satisfaction. Documentation in the medical record is essential for physicians to prove that the discussion for consent took place. If a patient suspects that a doctor is withholding information critical to giving proper consent, it is best to find another doctor.

Let's now explore how trust can be challenged in a crisis. With the arrival of the coronavirus, freshly minted doctors found themselves having to get out of their comfort zone and pitch in where they felt unprepared. Up to that point, their education was fairly predictable. They had trust in their mentors and the setting for their training, usually a hospital with appropriate supervision. A controlled learning environment allowed them to consume small bites of medical experience within a teaching institution. Once the

COVID-19 floodgates opened and the residents-in-training were called on to assume responsibilities few had anticipated, the scenarios created significant anxiety. Personal protective equipment (PPE) was scarce. How would they perform under stress? How could they learn what they needed to know to care for patients in a crisis? They would draw on inner strengths, on knowledge they had accumulated and on their compassion for people in need. Like drinking from a fire hose, these young doctors had to adapt to their unfamiliar environment. Resourcefully, they used their familiar tools to deal with a flood of information and unfamiliar situations. For example, the young doctors went to YouTube and learned how to set up ventilators. The coronavirus crisis created life and death events, considered outliers in their education before the pandemic.[17] One of the most poignant essays written by a resident-in-training dealt with notifying patients of their positive results for COVID-19 infection.[18] Carolyn Schulman, MD, a third-year resident in emergency medicine in Washington, DC, had to deal with the emotional distress of those on the phone, including her own mother who tested positive for the virus. Dr. Schulman learned some valuable lessons about dealing with patients' fears, anger, and need for emotional support. She served as a trusting voice at a time of extreme stress for those she called. It is also remarkable that her assignment included asking the patients whether they would accept follow-up questions as part of ongoing research on COVID-19. "I have a script of questions for every patient I call, asking whether they are willing to receive future calls for research purposes. All reply with an emphatic, "Yes, anything I can do to help."

Not all stories emanating from the pandemic inspired trust. KevinMD posted many examples of the frustration that frontline workers experienced due to the overwhelming tragedies played out during exhausting shifts. Some were told by their administrators not to wear their protective masks because of the chance of inducing fear in patients. Really! Cries for more protective equipment appeared not to be heard. Healthcare workers were given gag orders not to talk to the media, because negative comments would reflect poorly on the hospital. These conditions worked against the values of the doctors and nurses caring for the gravely ill, patients whose illness could result in the deaths of their caregivers. Multiple stories spoke to young couples drawing up wills and creating videos of their final words if things did not work out for them. Fear was nearly as contagious as the virus. The trust healthcare workers had placed in their employers seemed misplaced, indeed.

The President's Coronavirus Task Force gave daily briefings regarding the data accumulated on coronavirus infections and the projections for disease models that were changing constantly. Much of what Drs. Birx and Fauci spoke about was technical, but their words provided some caution and reassurance at the same time. These specialists in public health and immunology gave us a realistic picture of the threat posed by this silent killer and what measures we should take to prevent spread of the infection. Not all information available to the public was as reliable, however. In fact, the public's trust was degraded by contradictory statements coming from social media and other sources. "Do this, don't do that, unless you must do that" became part of the shtick of comediennes, including a hilarious faux press conference by Anne-Britt Schenk.[19] I sent the video by text to my friends and family, much to their delight. Laughing helped to blow off some of the steam of the stress we were all feeling.

Some rumors regarding hoarding of scarce equipment and price gouging for their sales garnered the attention of reporters. A doctor was arrested for promoting a vitamin treatment as a cure for COVID-19. Distributors of healthcare products desperately needed in this country attempted to sell them abroad for a much greater profit and were stopped by the Justice Department. The CARES Act, passed by Congress and signed into law by the President to help small businesses and families suffering economic damage from the shutdown, got off to a slow start. Our questions about the reliability of government to meet the needs of people in an emergency became more frequent and intense. While private industry stepped up to the challenge of rapidly manufacturing ventilators and masks and of meeting other supply needs, it became clear that we were unprepared for a pandemic. Some of the delay in knowing the extent of the contagion resulted from faulty test kits originating from the Centers for Disease Control and Prevention. We searched for answers to questions about the pandemic without any comparable examples in our recent history. The SARS and Ebola viruses arose in foreign lands, as did the virus that produced COVID-19. However, we became complacent in our attitudes toward risk of a pandemic because the spread of these former pathogens had been relatively contained. The spread of the coronavirus took off at an exponential rate before we could do much to stop it.

While there was little medical treatment available for COVID-19 in the early appearance of the epidemic other than support (e.g., oxygen, isolation, prevention of fluid overload), there was an abundance of help from good Samaritans for those at greatest risk. Americans are a generous people. They sewed cloth masks, they retrofitted as ventilators the apparatus for treating sleep apnea, and they delivered groceries to confined populations. My wife and I dropped off food and held up our dog so that my mother-in-law, who resides in an independent living home for older adults, could see him through her window. We were strictly prohibited from visiting her in her apartment. She was fortunate that there were no infections in either the residents or the staff in her facility. Other facilities for older people, in New Hampshire and elsewhere, have not been so lucky. And we're not out of the woods, yet.

Chapter 3

Past History

A GOOD STORY is memorable for its heroes and villains. Even before there was the printed word, stories were told for their entertainment value and for offering moral lessons to the audience. The events I am about to share deal with true characters whose names are part of the public record. Virtues and flaws are part of the spectrum of human behavior, and it so happens that my medical specialty of ophthalmology was featured at both ends of the spectrum.

Li Wenlaing, MD, was a 33-year-old ophthalmologist practicing at Wuhan Central Hospital in China. I learned about his death from my American Academy of Ophthalmology newsfeed dated February 10, 2020. It read, "Coronavirus kills Chinese whistleblower ophthalmologist." I had read about some of the backstory before his hospitalization and rapid decline on social media. After he posted his comments on a cluster of SARS-like pneumonia cases he had encountered in late December 2019, the information was widely circulated. He was confronted by Chinese officials and forced to sign a paper claiming that he made "false comments" that had "severely disturbed the social order." A copy of that letter was later posted on Weibo. After he returned to work, Dr. Li contracted COVID-19 from an asymptomatic patient in his eye clinic. Tests confirmed that he was infected with the coronavirus on January 31, 2020. As his symptoms worsened, he was hospitalized, ultimately succumbing to the disease on

February 7. The news article went on to describe how his death had affected his nation and his specialty society.[20]

"The news of his demise has sparked a public outpouring of anger and grief. Many have hailed him a martyr and a national hero for his attempts to warn the public." It took great courage for Dr. Li to openly describe to his colleagues what he had observed about the new cases of pneumonia and the associated risk of possible transmission of an infectious agent. His commitment to the truth ultimately cost him his life. His medical specialty society paid tribute to his efforts to inform the public. His loss was a crushing blow to the pursuit of truth by a respected physician. Although Chinese officials later retracted the letter of confession, their initial actions condemning the doctor reinforced for many Americans (and for foreign observers) distrust of the Communist Party apparatus and its enabling by the World Health Organization.[21] Questions arising from the early denial of the threat of spread by officials undermined our trust in political leaders and institutions responsible for public health.[22]

With rare exception, surveys of the public show a high regard for physicians and their work. However, the exceptional cases of physician impairment and misconduct, adversely affecting the safety of the public, command extraordinary media attention. Boards of Registration in Medicine are responsible for granting licensure to doctors with the requirement to perform their duties with professional integrity. These organizations are composed of doctors, lawyers, administrators and laypeople charged with hearing complaints of alleged behavior that could jeopardize the public safety. Often, if the doctor comes forward and seeks help, for example in treatment for alcohol abuse, the matter is dealt with in confidence. Reinstatement of the doctor's license depends on the individual circumstances and proof of rehabilitation (e.g., urine tests for drugs). In egregious cases of a physician's blatant disregard for the duties and responsibilities required of the medical profession, the doctor can be sanctioned by the courts. Such a case occurred recently in California.

A prominent ophthalmologist serving as dean of a medical school, who admittedly suffered from mental illness, behaved in a manor so repugnant that the Administrative Court judge found in favor of the Board of Medicine to revoke the doctor's license to practice medicine.[23] It was determined that the doctor used illicit drugs, prescribed drugs to his mistress and himself, enticed the use of illicit drugs (including methamphetamine and heroin) by a minor and acted to undo the drug abstinence program of his associates by offering drugs. The judge's finding was made after weighing complaints by the Board and hearing testimony from the doctor. The written decision runs 63 pages. Perhaps the most egregious act of the doctor, described by a *Los Angeles Times* reporter[24] and cited in the judge's decision, was his failure to perform like a doctor when his companion overdosed on drugs. "His failure to seek appropriate treatment... when she suffered an overdose and his misstatements to medical personnel constitute shocking behavior by a physician," the judge wrote.

Cases of physician impairment this extreme are unusual, but they weigh heavily on the public's trust in doctors in general. With Boards of Registration acting in good faith, a balancing act must be created to respect the reputation of the doctor as complaints are investigated by due process. If overzealous, Boards may scar doctors in their efforts to meet their professional obligations after admitting wrongdoing. The key factors requiring forgiveness and restitution include an honest admission of the error and a plan for recovery. In an ideal world, a balance is struck between allowing a caring, competent physician to remain in practice, while having met concerns for public safety. But we don't live in an ideal world, do we?

You may have heard the proverb, "one rotten apple spoils the barrel." In the example given above, according to expert medical testimony, the doctor showed insufficient remorse for his behavior and posed a risk to the public despite attending a rehab program and receiving counseling. Revoking his medical license was appropriate, given the evidence presented. Weeding out dangerous doctors is necessary in such cases. In this particular case, the doctor claimed that he suffered from a hypomanic condition that was part of a mental illness characterized by bipolar II disorder. What that designation means, according to the psychiatrists' manual[25], is depression aggravated by manic (or near manic) behavior, often associated with substance abuse.

Despite such extreme examples of physicians who lost their way, the public wants to trust its doctors. You may ask yourself, how much mental illness and aberrant behavior among physicians can society accept, assuming proper treatment is ongoing and the doctor is deemed not a risk to the safety of patients? Is a single episode of postpartum depression something that should exclude a doctor from practice? Is it fair to ask a doctor who long ago was treated for such depression to divulge that history when seeking hospital privileges? Should the standard for mental stability and competence to practice medicine hinge on such a singular event in an otherwise spotless professional career? When does burnout become depression, and what can be done to prevent it from taking over a doctor's life? These are not simply rhetorical questions. They arise from case histories that are detailed in a special edition of *Qualitative Research in Medicine and Healthcare* on physician mental health. In *"Winding Down, Facing Up: Insights Gained on the Road to Retirement,"* [26] I described the funk I was in near the end of my medical career, and how I emerged from that negative state of mind. I addressed issues raised in experiencing burnout, leaving a medical practice, and finding another calling. Fortunately, I was able to turn around things in my head and my attitude with counseling and without antidepressants. My case demonstrates that a message of hope and of redirection of professional energy can result in the lifting of a dark mood and gaining a new purpose and source of pride. Writing has filled that gap for me, something I needed going forward after leaving medical practice.

The guest editorial in that issue of *Qualitative Research in Medicine and Healthcare* written by Pamela Wible, MD, highlighted the changes adopted by the Federation of State Medical Boards to remove questions from licensing applications that may violate the Americans With Disabilities Act. New Hampshire's Board just this year modified its applications for licensure to eliminate questions that would force some physicians to lie about past behavior for fear that their application would be rejected over mental health issues. These welcome changes help to remove some of the stigma of mental illness in physicians. How physicians live up to the standards of practice should guide the process of attestation required by hospital credentials committees. You could say it should demonstrate a process of "trust, but verify."

In the course of evaluating such applications for licensure and/or hospital credentials, the National Data Bank is queried regarding any malpractice suits pending or adjudicated. It is the responsibility of these committees to look into potential patterns of bad judgment or poor performance by physicians. Medicare publishes notices of doctors convicted of fraud and abuse, but even these references are not completely without prejudice. Recently, an article[27] described how a difference of opinion regarding the medical necessity for inserting stents in coronary arteries landed a cardiologist in jail. He was released after serving nine months of a lengthy sentence when his conviction was overturned on appeal. A panel of cardiologists assembled by Medicare for the purpose of uncovering suspected abuse led to charges of unnecessarily placing stents for narrowing of the heart vessels. However, the federal agency failed to disclose exculpatory evidence to the defense that the variance in indications for the surgical intervention was, in fact, only 7%. "A trio of government doctors said that between 21% and 50% of the cases they reviewed showed unnecessary stents. The government called this a 'pattern' that proved Dr. Paulus was a criminal." It was a difference of opinion that landed the doctor in prison, and the federal government lost the case on appeal.

Doctors who scam the system, who receive illegal kickbacks and who injure patients due to negligence deserve to suffer consequences. However, another proverb that comes to mind is, "don't throw the baby out with the bath water." Avoid the error of eliminating something good when attempting to get rid of something bad.

The struggle for balance in decisions made either by the Board of Medicine or by committees evaluating applications in medical specialties can show significant collateral damage. Consider the tragic story of the suicide of a young physician.[28] "Early in life, Leigh struggled with alcoholism and drug use, both of which she used to cope with depression and anxiety. She spent many of her formative years either intoxicated or incarcerated until she finally enrolled in an intensive recovery program. It was during this period of clarity and self-awareness that she decided on medicine as a path to redemption."

The doctor had openly admitted her history of alcohol and drug dependence, and she managed to remain sober and to work hard in her studies. She attended medical school. She performed well and was well liked by her peers and faculty. However, her dream of becoming an orthopedic surgeon was blocked by her history of alcohol and drug abuse. After two unsuccessful attempts to land a residency program in orthopedics, and despite performing well in her surgery residency, she took her own life because she believed that she could never achieve her goal. Her friend, Candy Ezimora, MD, describes how devastated she was to learn of Leigh's death and what it meant for the medical profession.

"Despite all her accomplishments, accolades, and commendations, Leigh could not escape her past. Instead of offering support and allowing this incredible woman the opportunity to become an outstanding physician, the medical education system rejected her. It continued to punish her for mistakes made long ago, misdeeds she had more than repented for. What more could she have done? How much more was she expected to give before she would be accepted into this profession and allowed to do what she so desperately yearned to?" My heart was broken to read the deceased doctor's final words. "Please. Make my life, and my death, mean something. Something for someone else. This is my hope."

We should create an environment in healthcare in which doctors who need help can get help without recrimination. We must also look at how our current environment in healthcare shows a fracture among thought leaders, something I refer to as parallel thinking.[29]

Parallel Thinking Won't Solve Problems in Healthcare

A lot of media attention, including television, print and online sources, is focused on various plans to revolutionize the delivery of healthcare in America. Critics point to medical errors, waste of resources and lack of access among the numerous factors requiring the replacement of our healthcare system. To many politicians and think tank experts, the combination of government support programs (including Medicare, Medicaid and Social Security disability) plus private group- and commercial health insurance plans no longer meet the needs of the people. These proposed replacement systems, which are estimated to cost trillions of dollars, would further undermine the relationships doctors have with their patients due to the heavy hand of government. Furthermore, none of the proposed delivery solutions speaks to the disturbing trend of physician burnout and the associated physician shortage that the country will face in the future. Currently, these parallel lines of policy do not intersect, and physicians are feeling the stress of uncertainty regarding their roles in an ever-changing healthcare landscape.

In addition to their primary role as healers, doctors are now expected to be data entry experts. Their work product and reimbursement are justified by the diagnostic and procedure codes documented in the medical record. The requirement for documentation shortens the time doctors spend with each patient, and the requisite computer entries seem to take precedence over patient care. The result is a growing dissatisfaction with the practice of medicine and feelings of depersonalization.

Physician depression and suicide are now major topics of investigation and comment in professional journals, yet the notion of parallel thinking on the subject of physician well being has become apparent. One school of thought believes that the doctor needs to become more reflective and resilient in the practice of modern medicine. According to this school, the system in which the physician works and lives must provide the tools (e.g., yoga and discussion groups) to help strike a balance between the commitments of professional and personal time. An opposing view looks at the world in which doctors are educated and employed as adversarial, decrying the violation of doctors' human rights due to sleep deprivation, harassment and irregular breaks from work. Such a system, according to some physician advocates, blames the victims for the abuses it heaps upon doctors. When doctors feel there is nowhere to turn for help, they become depressed, some to the point of suicide.

The struggle to define a doctor's role in healthcare policy and practice must find some accommodation between the demands of the established administrative hierarchy and the individual physician's needs. Voices from each camp must be willing to listen and to engage each other in constructive dialogue. If the energy derived from opposing forces can be harnessed toward progress, a crisis in the delivery of healthcare may be averted. Let's try synergistic thinking, rather than parallel thinking, to tackle problems in healthcare.

This book will hopefully serve that goal.

Chapter 4

Medications

IN THIS CHAPTER, I offer a symbolic look at the stuff that sustains us and our healthcare, like vital medication. The difference, however, for purposes of evaluating trust in healthcare and its participants, relates to the information we derive every day from numerous sources. An astute reader will have noted the reference I made in the prior chapter on physician mental health, specifically my receiving counseling for burnout. Yes, I had a single session with a psychologist who specialized in offering cognitive behavioral therapy to treat doctors suffering the adverse effects of professional burnout. My analogy to this brief encounter with therapy is the answer given by candidate for US President, Bill Clinton. When asked in the 1992 presidential campaign if he had ever used marijuana (something that tended to separate his generation from that of his opponent's), he admitted that, "I smoked it, but I didn't inhale." The discussion I had with the therapist gave me a perspective I had not considered while I was in the midst of winding down my medical career as an eye surgeon. She suggested that I take up writing because of my insights gained as a doctor and my continued desire to help others. Thanks to my sole (perhaps the word "soul" might be more accurate) therapy session, I constructed an image of retirement that would take on a new dimension for service. I would advocate for doctors and patients in a new way. I decided to build a website **www.paulpendermd.com**.

I developed a blog and linked my stories to other social media platforms. It was through my writings that the Chief Executive Officer for a healthcare start-up contacted me and invited me to advise his company on issues that impact patient care (much more coming on that in the chapter on Assessment and Plan). What I concluded from my therapy session is that I am not alone. In the survey mentioned earlier, nearly half of all the doctors polled had experienced symptoms of burnout (all specialties included with 15,000 respondents). As a surgeon and control freak, I had to find a way to face my new environment—not with uncertainty, but with purpose.

Reading Angela Duckworth's book, *Grit: The Power of Passion and Perseverance*, gave me an important reference for my next career stage. Her description of the value of cognitive behavioral therapy made me realize just how important it is to find solutions to mental roadblocks[30].

"Cognitive behavioral therapy—which aims to treat depression and other psychological maladies by helping patients think more objectively and behave in healthier ways—has shown that, whatever our childhood sufferings, we can generally learn to observe our negative self-talk and change our maladaptive behaviors. As with any other skill, we can practice interpreting what happens to us and respond as an optimist would. Cognitive behavioral therapy is now a widely practiced psychotherapeutic treatment for depression, and has proven longer-lasting in its effects than antidepressant medication."

Dr. Duckworth has studied the characteristics that lead to achieving personal and societal goals. Genes, talent and environment all contribute to grit, but the major determinants include passion, practice and persistence. Leaders in healthcare would be wise to take her advice as they tackle major challenges following the coronavirus pandemic.

We depend on solid information to make good judgments, but not all information that we receive through multiple channels meet the criteria for reliability. The *Harvard Gazette* recently featured faculty essays from the Kennedy school regarding the veracity of news material and the interpretation of facts. The writers represent a *Who's Who* of political analysts and social scientists, including those with progressive roots and others with conservative backgrounds. Nancy Gibbs, a former *Time* magazine editor, had this to say about the subject of democracy and the pursuit of truth in the presence of distrust[31].

"The twin crises of truth and trust are inseparable, making all the challenges of public policy that much more difficult to address. A Pew Research Center study found that two-thirds of Americans think that other Americans have little or no trust in the federal government; a majority believe that trust in individuals as well as institutions is shrinking, and that this will make it harder to solve the nation's problems. An insidious process is at work here: The very awareness of distrust and growing cynicism about government's ability to promote progress leads to disengagement. The more people turn away from a common public sphere to their own curated information streams, the greater the likelihood of political conflict, division, and misunderstanding."

I find it hard to disagree with the statement Ms. Gibbs makes. As we curate information from various sources, we may be exercising confirmation bias in our searches, going to places for opinions with which we already agree. Furthermore, the use of inflammatory statements, tweets and social media forms of condemnation tends to obscure the truth. We are bombarded by information designed to release neurotransmitters in our brains that are targeted toward addictions[32]. Arthur C. Brooks, former head of the American Enterprise Institute, describes the social media platforms on any contentious subject as "contempt machines."[33] It requires effort to sift and sort information in the digital age. It has created apprehension on the part of those fully engaged in social media.[34]

The Grip of Our Mobile Devices on Our Collective Consciousness

During a recent walk at Crystal Cove, a splendid California State Park with miles of pristine coastline, I encountered two young women sitting on a bench with a magnificent view of the ocean. Yet their only view of interest was their cell phone screens. One of them lifted her head long enough to say, 'Your dog is cute,' then returned to the rapture of her device. I thanked her and sat on an adjacent bench, directing my dog to the shade. I was curious about what was so significant as to capture such complete attention. Heads bowed, both young women remained motionless. Whales and dolphins swam a quarter mile offshore, and sea birds flocked in the wind currents. While I sat, I felt blessed to be experiencing the sights, sounds and scents of the ocean at low tide. The girls on the bench didn't know what they were missing. Or did they know, and not care? Was their obsession with their devices so great that they chose not to allow their minds to come up for air?

By most accounts, I am old enough to have lived through much of the information revolution. My first exposure to television was a 10-inch black and white set my parents acquired in 1954. The screen on my iPad is bigger than that original TV set. Technology has given greater convenience and entertainment options for more people than in any other generation. The Internet morphed from a Defense Department experiment to an always-on source of information, accessible to literally billions of people. However, there is a dark side to the influence of such technology, especially when it comes to social media.

An article dated Wednesday, April 24, 2019, in the *Wall Street Journal* section on Technology and Media featured a profile of Tristan Harris. The headline reads, "Tech's Gadfly Reboots Warning." The author, Betsy Morris, describes Harris as the conscience of Silicon Valley. Harris has crusaded to bring greater awareness of the addictive potential of social media and smartphones. "As we've been upgrading machines, we've been downgrading humanity," he says. Harris should know—he was a product designer for Google before issuing his warning about the advertising model that has driven the growth of so many Internet companies. In the days before social media, ads were part of mass media, delivering messages that resonated with the target demographic. Marlboro cigarettes featured the Marlboro Man, a cowboy who exuded masculinity. "Smoke this brand and become a real man," was the not-so-subtle message. Thanks to Facebook and other social media, companies can more carefully target users' information collected online. A user's satisfaction or lack thereof associated with a product or service is instantly circulated among other users or 'friends.' Teenagers already lacking in confidence are more likely to feel the effects of group pressure, especially when it can be applied remotely through the device they are holding. According to Harris, "We have to go from being really, really sophisticated about technology to being really, really sophisticated about human behavior."

Teenagers seek acceptance from their peers. Social media preys upon their insecurities. Fear of Missing Out drives their addiction to their devices. Features designed to attract and keep users' attention have become common-place. Becoming 'part of the conversation' has allowed Twitter's stock to increase by 16% in the first quarter this year. And it seems everyone has an opinion. But as one financial advisor observed, the Internet has provided, for those with nothing to say, a place to say it.

The Internet offers information for a price. The cost of distraction and the exclusion of life experience can be high, indeed. Our smartphones are wonderful tools, but with unlimited use their effects on our psyche can be profound. Texting while driving has been associated with numerous fatalities, most often linked to teen use of cellphones.

What will it take to flip the switch, to allow device users to put them away and to smell the roses before they wilt? In my opinion, it will take other aspects in our lives that give us joy. The endorphin release from exercise, the per-ception of the beauty of nature, the pleasurable passage from a piece of good writing, and a face-to-face conversa-tion with trusted friends all contribute to a sense of well-being. Just as our bodies require sleep, our psyches require respite from the constant barrage of online information and images. Recognizing the addictive potential of device use is the first step toward regaining control. Our minds deserve as much.

I broadened my education by learning what some social media influencers are thinking about the issue of trust. I read an interview from *Michigan Today*[35] with Jia Tolentino, whose book *Trick Mirror: Reflections on Self-Delusion*[36] was recently published to rave reviews. She writes for the *New Yorker* and is considered a spokesperson for the millennial generation. The subtitle of her book is revealing. Self-delusion is part of the currency of social media, and cynicism is a byproduct. She speaks of her avatar, the image one wants to project online. Her observation for maintaining an online presence is a blend of hype and narcissism.

"In real life, you can walk around living life and be visible to other people. But you can't just walk around and be visible on the internet—for anyone to see you, you have to *act*. You have to communicate in order to maintain an internet presence. And, because the internet's central platforms are built around personal profiles, it can seem—first at a mechanical level, and later on as an encoded instinct—like the main purpose of this communication is to make yourself look good."

Ms. Tolentino's take on social media in the age of COVID-19 is less subject to the distortions of a trick mirror. The following excerpt is taken from her interview with *Michigan Today*.

"One thing I find promising is that a fundamental

premise of the identity economy (that it's good and interesting and perpetually monetizable to have people performing an attractive version of their lives to one another) is looking especially stupid right now. No one wants to see celebrities in their mansions talking about wellness routines. No one wants to see influencers posting photos of themselves in beautiful, novel environments, because that means they left the house." Returning to her book, I was struck by the example she cited of fraud and deception perpetrated by Elizabeth Holmes, the former CEO of Theranos. At one time, she was considered the youngest woman self-made billionaire to ever walk the planet. According to Ms. Tolentino, "The con is in the DNA of this country, which was founded on the idea that it is good, important, and even noble to see an opportunity to profit and take whatever you can." Holmes founded Theranos as a tech company designed to obtain vast analyses of blood components from a simple finger stick. Her device never fully materialized. She faked lab results and bilked millions of dollars from investors to keep the scam going. Finally, after her exploits were exposed by John Carreyrou[37], an investigative reporter for the *Wall Street Journal*, Holmes was indicted by a grand jury on nine counts of fraud. She kept the charade going for more than a dozen years before being caught. Ms. Tolentino concludes her description of the rise and fall of this young entrepreneur, not as a tragic figure, but rather as a representative of the corruption caused by capitalism. "The absurd length of time that it took for Holmes to be exposed illuminates a grim, definitive truth of our era: scammers are always safest at the top."

What gives rise to such cynicism? Is Ms Tolentino's generation the only one to suffer economic hardship? From the perspective of young people born after 1980, recessions were the rule, not the exception. The year 2000 brought a burst to the dot.com bubble. The financial crisis of 2008 gave rise to poor prospects for employment, even with a college degree in hand. Those who found jobs were thrilled to have employer-sponsored health insurance, a topic discussed in much greater detail in Chapter 10. Rumblings heard for a federal government-sponsored health plan to insure everyone are not new, but the economic disappointments felt by the millennials fuel their mindset.

As part of our daily dose of information medication, consider this snapshot of the patterns of care currently in use in America. When we have questions on healthcare, especially for perceived personal health issues, we seek answers from various sources. For access to answers, we have emergency care, urgent care, routine (outpatient) or maintenance care, inpatient hospital care, convalescent care, Veterans Administration care, residences for older adults (as independent living or assisted living), complementary medical care (non-allopathic or herb-derived), mental health care, elective surgical care, employer-sponsored care, telehealth conferencing, internet-sourced-mail-order-care (for conditions like erectile dysfunction and hair loss) and no care at all. Each topic could fill many books. Although I will not dwell on these spokes of the healthcare wheel, in the center of the spokes stands the hub, the Big Kahuna that comprises the entitlement programs of Medicare, Medicaid and the health insurance exchanges created by the Patient Protection and Affordable

Care Act of 2010, otherwise known as Obamacare (much more on this in the chapter on Review of Systems). However, this list of elements that compose the patchwork of our healthcare system gives you an idea just how complex our delivery system has become. The fact that the apparatus malfunctions should not come as a surprise. It should also be apparent that the level of a person's medical knowledge, assumed by various gatekeepers to access, is not uniform. Not all patients read what their health plan covers or know what symptoms constitute a true medical emergency.

Laws governing what level of medical knowledge is assumed by the "prudent layperson" for seeking appropriate care add to the confusion.[38]

Prudent Layperson Standard Should Apply to Urgent Care Centers

An emergency physician, LS, came to me for an eye problem. After diagnosing and treating him, we talked about his current assignments. He covers hospital emergency rooms in two towns and the urgent care centers affiliated with the parent hospital. Lately, he has had to tell patients in an urgent care setting that a study, like a CT scan, is medically indicated, but he does not know if the patient's insurance will deny the claim. For example, a 65-year-old gentleman 'bashed his head' and LS told him that the standard of care is to get a CT scan of the head. However, the patient was confused when LS said that the patient's insurance would not authorize the test. The medical reviewer, seated at his desk in suburban Chicago, by telephone denied the authorization because the test should be done at the Emergency Room of the hospital. The logic did not inspire me, so I asked if that were an unusual situation, having to get prior authorization for a CT scan in an Urgent Care center. Authorization is being denied because the patient did not self-refer appropriately. Submitted claims are being denied after the fact. The insurance industry has paid increasing numbers of claims for studies done in an Emergency Room setting with the passage of a national law that uses the standard of the "prudent layperson" who should be covered for symptoms that would reasonably prompt someone to seek immediate attention. Unfortunately, the insurance companies now are asserting that such symptoms, presented to an Urgent Care center, do not meet the standard of the 'prudent layperson.' This approach puts an undue burden on the patient to judge the severity of his or her symptoms and to self-refer to what insurance companies consider 'appropriate' settings. Is this reasonable? The patient, unless connected with the medical field, is in no position to know just how serious his or her symptoms may be. Denials for authorization for CT scans allow insurance companies to limit their 'losses,' that is, paying claims. There are ethical and legal questions raised by this policy of denying claims. Are financial incentives offered to medical reviewers to deny such claims? Should not the 'prudent layperson' standard be applied no matter the setting in which the patient seeks care for an urgent problem? Is there medical liability for the ER doctor who fails to order the test when such test is not authorized by the insurance company's medical reviewer? See the statement from the American College of Emergency Physicians.[39]

The initial purpose of Urgent Care centers was to provide the public with simple care for simple medical problems, e.g., minor cuts, sprains, colds and the like. However, since their geographic location filled a niche in the community, Urgent Care centers have come to serve the function of hospital Emergency Rooms without the wait. Electronic billboards boast the shorter waiting times to receive care in Urgent Care centers compared to the parent Hospital Emergency Room. Who wouldn't go to where you can be seen more quickly for your problem? It took Federal law in 1997 to require insurance companies to apply a 'prudent layperson' standard for paying claims derived from Emergency Room care. The same standard should apply to claims derived from Urgent Care centers. Either that, or insurance companies, AT THEIR EXPENSE, must educate the public on the severity of a multitude of symptoms that would otherwise require a degree in medicine.

The coronavirus pandemic has prompted healthcare companies to consider the intersection of urgent care and telemedicine. In a recent podcast,[40] Dr. Stephen Klasko, CEO of Thomas Jefferson University and Jefferson Health, described his program's decade-long investment in telehealth. As one of telemedicine's pioneers, Jefferson Health developed a mobile app for its subscribers to remove some of the pressure on its emergency room. Jefferson Health offers discounts to members who first consult their mobile app before coming to the emergency room. That incentive to members saved the healthcare system millions of dollars in emergency room costs. Similarly, Detroit's Henry Ford

Hospital and Medical Center envisions a broader use of telehealth to streamline access to its urgent care centers, as a recent AMA podcast demonstrated.[41]

The future of healthcare delivery will show that collecting and transmitting pertinent individual medical information to prompt the appropriate access point to care will save money and time. It will also help patients navigate the shoals of confusion when the stress of an illness may seem overwhelming.

Chapter 5

Allergies

IN THE HUMAN BODY, we know that there are genetic predispositions and environmental exposures for intolerance to various substances, whether it is to lactose, peanuts or poison ivy. Inability to tolerate things can be extreme, such as when a susceptible person eats shellfish, resulting in a complete collapse of the circulatory system. Such an allergic response, called anaphylactic shock, may occur from a bee sting if a body has had a previous exposure to the venom and now has an "immune memory" of it. The best way to escape a possible fatality, besides keeping an injection of adrenaline handy, is to avoid at all costs exposure to the antigen. Staying away from potentially deadly exposures is the general rule that governs our survival.

Such a principle of avoidance appears among policymakers for healthcare. In my experience, it results from legislators avoiding the subject of expanding scope of practice for healthcare professionals. Most legislators are not, themselves, healthcare professionals. They would prefer not politicizing differences in the training of doctors, nurse practitioners, physician assistants and others when attempting to bridge gaps in healthcare delivery. The concept of "supervision" of limited-license practitioners (defined by laws in each state) by physicians with a medical degree smacks of paternalism to many participants in the delivery of healthcare. Hearing the voices of non-physicians lobbying for expansion of their roles in healthcare, policymakers have come to believe that there is little difference between primary care physicians and nurse practitioners for rendering preventive or "routine" care. Such thinking is offensive to doctors who tout their broader educational background and intensity of experience for diagnosis and treatment. While their ranks continue to decline from retirement and from attrition due to the demands of regulators, physicians will continue to voice their objections to what they feel are watered down proposals for quality care. Quality should drive the search for solutions to the anticipated doctor shortage. Convenience for patients means little if adverse health conditions are not suspected and diagnosed in time. Despite the objections of organized medicine, some states have already moved to expand the scope of practice of limited-license professionals by legislative fiat without the requisite supervised training.

Academic policy analysts have weighed in on the debate over licensing requirements for healthcare workers within state legislatures. Florida has recently relaxed requirements for education and training as a response to pressures from the coronavirus pandemic. The authors of an op-ed in the *Wall Street Journal* recommend that the temporary waiving of requirements should be made permanent.[42]

"Florida's recent reforms are expanding the range of services that advanced practice professionals may provide and eliminating direct-supervision requirements. Pharmacists in Florida will be able to test for common illnesses like strep throat and the flu. Other states should follow suit to lend greater flexibility to health-care providers and allow physicians to focus on caring for the patients in greatest need."

"While most states are adopting these reforms temporarily in response to the coronavirus crisis, there is no reason they shouldn't consider permanently rolling back unnecessary regulations that limit access to care."

Unnecessary regulations? I don't believe so. It is not simply a matter of defending doctors' turf that these regulations are part of state laws. They are designed to ensure public safety. In my capacity as President of the NH Society of Eye Physicians and Surgeons, I have testified before legislative committees in both the NH House and Senate to uphold the "gold standard" of a medical degree for treating sight-threatening conditions. From my perspective as a physician specializing in the medical and surgical treatment of eye diseases, expanding the scope of practice for optometry without commensurate education and requisite training does not appear to be in the public interest. For me and for many other physicians, broadening the range of privileges for independent healthcare workers without requiring additional training and supervision appears to cut corners to care.

Is this an argument for fractionalism among healthcare workers? Not if affiliations become formalized with physicians of distinction leading the way (discussed in Chapter 10). The way forward to rebuilding trust in healthcare involves teamwork with the patient at the center of the enterprise.

Chapter 6

Social History

TRUST IS A SOCIAL CONSTRUCT, the appreciation of honesty and good intentions between people. I begin this chapter with some of the provisions of the Patient Protection and Affordable Care Act (referred to as the ACA) of 2010 in terms of their impact on diverse populations in America. The intention of the designers of the ACA was to cover the uninsured, a population already subject to health disparities long before the onset of the coronavirus pandemic. There is still much to learn about the ways in which the virus preferentially attacked minorities and the elderly, but I will attempt to put together some of the puzzle pieces from what we do know. Such an analysis can inform ways to help reduce health disparities, an issue at the heart of rebuilding trust in healthcare.

In my opinion, one of the most significant papers[43] to come out of the Kaiser Family Foundation, published in November 2015, dealt with Medicaid and the uninsured. The authors of the paper, a family physician and a policy director at the Kaiser Family Foundation, entitled their position paper, *"Beyond Health Care: The Role of Social Determinants in Promoting Health and Health Equity."* The paper listed the many ways in which the ACA and Medicaid helped underserved communities. Citing examples of how community organizations funded by the ACA improved health by promoting health classes, better access to healthy food, and improved housing, the authors came to these conclusions:[44]

"The ACA provides a key opportunity to help improve access to care and reduce longstanding disparities faced by historically underserved populations through both its coverage expansions and provisions to help bridge health care and community health. To date, millions of Americans have gained coverage through the ACA coverage expansions, including many individuals from low-income, racial and ethnic minority, and other vulnerable communities who have faced longstanding disparities in coverage. However, research demonstrates that coverage alone is not enough to improve health outcomes and achieve health equity. There is growing recognition of the importance of not only integrating and coordinating services across providers and settings within the health care system, but also connecting and integrating health care with social supports and services that address the broad range of social and environmental factors that impact individuals' and communities' health and well-being."

The authors go on to recommend that a discussion of healthcare must be set in the context of the communities in which people live. Healthcare disparities, derived from social determinants of health, cannot be ignored.

"Looking ahead, framing health through a broader context to include factors related to the communities in which people are born, grow, live, work and age and learning from current initiatives will contribute to increased knowledge of how to achieve broader improvements in health and greater health equity."

Five years have passed since the paper was written, and 10 years have gone by since the ACA was passed. So where are we now? Progress in reducing disparities has been slow, contributing to distrust in government solutions. Furthermore, the coronavirus pandemic underscored the disparities that the ACA attempted to fix. The following quotes are taken from an interview[45] with Dr. James Hildreth, an African-American virologist who serves as President and CEO of Meharry Medical College in Nashville, Tennessee, one of the nation's largest historically black medical schools.

WSJ: "What are some of the lessons from your HIV research that apply to Covid-19?

Dr. Hildreth: "One of the biggest challenges then was a misperception that AIDS only impacted gay white men. At the time, politicians weren't too interested in solving problems related to homosexuality. One lesson for Covid-19 was that we had to quickly dispel any myths about the coronavirus so people would make the appropriate decisions. For a while, young people thought they were impervious, and that caused them to act irresponsibly. One thing I'm trying to do is make sure the science is out there for people to understand."

WSJ: "How might a bigger focus on the risk factors of the disease have changed the efforts to mitigate Covid-19?"

Dr. Hildreth: "China, after two months, noted that if you had diabetes, heart disease, hypertension or you smoked, or were elderly with underlying conditions, your likelihood of getting severe disease and dying was much higher. In the U.S., it's well-established that if you're from a minority group or you're poor, you're more likely to have those conditions and therefore more likely to have poorer outcomes."

"Knowing that, we should have been aggressively

proactive in testing around the most vulnerable populations. Think about nursing homes. People are being ravaged. With an appropriate national strategy, we could have made sure resources were in place to protect those most vulnerable."

Assessing the demographic characteristics of minority populations, Dr. Hildreth points out that multi-generational housing contributes to the spread of the coronavirus. Healthy-seeming young people who are asymptomatic carriers bring the virus home and infect their elderly relatives. Where minorities often work at jobs in close quarters and take public transportation to work, their chance for spread is greater than for those who can work at home and self-isolate. The interview concludes with important implications for gathering data on comorbidities, like diabetes, hypertension and asthma, along with racial statistics for better strategies for healthcare delivery.[46] It also shows why an institution like his is important for sending the right message to his community.

WSJ: "What role do health centers like yours play?"

Dr. Hildreth: "There are still quite a number of African-Americans who are skeptical and not trusting of any kind of test or messages being promulgated by certain institutions. That makes it really important for organizations like Meharry to be on the front lines delivering messages and providing care and services."

Organized medicine has taken up the issue of healthcare disparities by creating advocates within their ranks. The American Medical Association (AMA) established a set of principles for achieving health equity in their 2018 Annual Meeting. While organized medicine cannot be solely responsible for changing the healthcare system, it can influence decision-makers who can have that effect. The AMA recognizes that there are problems with no easy solutions.[47]

"The AMA acknowledged that physicians alone cannot control all factors necessary to achieve health equity. For some, the AMA's role will be identifying their importance and to urge those who can have a direct role to act. Most, if not all, determinants of health must be addressed in collaboration with others."

"To achieve health equity, the AMA outlined a framework approach for the sustained effort:
- Advocate for health care access, research, and data collection
- Promote equity in care
- Increase health workforce diversity and cultural awareness/competency
- Influence determinants of health
- Voice and model commitment to health equity."

In April 2019, the AMA announced that the position of Chief Health Equity Officer would be held by Althea Maybank, MD, MPH, formerly deputy commissioner with the New York City Department of Health and Mental Hygiene. She is a pediatrician board certified in preventive medicine/public health. In April 2020, Dr. Maybank made an impassioned plea for careful data collection on racial and ethnic features of the COVID-19 pandemic.[48]

"So far, less than a dozen states have publicly shared information on the racial and ethnic patterns of COVID-19. Yet what has emerged so far paints an alarming portrait."

"Michigan's newly released data raises particular alarm with a disproportionate percentage, 35% and 40% respectively, of cases and deaths happening among blacks. In Wisconsin's Milwaukee County, half of the cases and 81% of the deaths were amongst blacks, when blacks make up only a quarter of the population. In Chicago, seven in 10 COVID-related deaths were among blacks while blacks constitute less than one-third of the city's population."

Ensuring optimal health and fairness for all people in America is the goal. However, until adequate data are collected from public health agencies, including racial and ethnic factors, we will have an incomplete picture of how best to allocate resources for recovery from the pandemic.[49]

Several medical groups signed a letter to US Health and Human Services Secretary Alex Azar urging the collection and publication of data on those groups disproportionately affected by COVID-19. According to that letter, the information from public health officials may be ignored or misunderstood by people with limited English proficiency.[50]

"The letter, which is signed by the American Medical Association, the American Academy of Pediatrics, the American Academy of Family Physicians, the National Medical Association, the National Hispanic Medical Association, the Association of American Indian Physicians, and the National Council of Asian Pacific Islander Physicians, acknowledges that the Covid-19 pandemic did not create these inequities of care, but it has and will continue to severely exacerbate existing and alarming social inequities along racial and ethnic lines, e.g., in housing stability, in employment status, in healthcare access, and in food security."

Earlier in this discussion, the issue of housing was touched on in terms of density and multi-generational living. People employed in service industries may have less flexibility to self-isolate, living paycheck to paycheck. In his book *Food Fix*, Dr. Mark Hyman has documented food insecurity as a major component in the cause of many chronic diseases.[51] Obesity, diabetes, hypertension and heart disease are known risk factors for succumbing to COVID-19, conditions related in part to available foods and consumption of high-sugar content foods and beverages.

Metropolitan "hot spots" for coronavirus infection across the globe show certain features in common, according to a recent report.[52] High density of people, public transportation, chronic health conditions (including smoking) and advanced age all make for a deadly formula. The high percentage of deaths for COVID-19 positive cases in nursing homes and facilities for veterans in America speaks to confinement as an underlying enabler for the virus. In New Hampshire[53], by early May 2020 for example, positive cases for residents in nursing homes and independent living facilities numbered 473, but positive cases among staff tallied 266. This extreme ratio for positive COVID-19 test results prompted the governor to ban visitors to these types of facilities, even though restrictions were loosened for other populations in the state.

Some have argued that restrictions placed upon freedom of movement and assembly are extreme, given our current understanding of the spread of the coronavirus. Critics doubt the wisdom of mitigation efforts, especially in areas with relatively few reported cases. Not so, says

Kevin Cranston, Assistant Commissioner for the Massachusetts Bureau of Health. In a recent interview, he describes why reducing risk is so important, and how treating people with respect is essential to dealing with the pandemic. As a graduate of Harvard Divinity School and a gay man living and working in the age of HIV/AIDS, he understands the need for education of the public to reduce the risk of spreading the virus.[54] He speaks of the phases of the epidemic and our response, from early case identification and containment, to contact tracing in the development of community transmission.

"Each of these phases in the life of the epidemic has specific recommendations attached to them. When you have a small number of cases in a localized area, you are operating under the approach of containment, whereby you look to isolate a very small number of people and quarantine their close contacts to make sure they don't spread the disease. But as you move into these larger environments, or into what appears to be widespread community transmission, you move into some of the strategies we're seeing now—things like school closures, stay-at-home orders, restrictions on the size of groups, and cancellation of large events."

In May 2020, the CDC released a document with "decision trees" designed to allow the safe transition to reopening societal activities.[55] While governors of individual states have adopted different strategies for relaxing restrictions, the CDC guidelines remain the most reliable source of information as we emerge from the pandemic.

Distrust of healthcare information has inevitably led to divisions among Americans. In a recent interview with

Bret Baier of Fox News, Matthew McConaughey bemoaned the divisions over the coronavirus response.[56] In his opinion, two wars are at work here: one against the virus, and one between political parties. In such a scenario, we lose both wars. He believes that if we fight the virus together, and remain united in our collective efforts, we can beat the virus. He has funded through his foundation public service announcements that support a unified effort in dealing with the pandemic. Until the science "catches up," our due diligence requires working toward the common good and putting aside political differences. Easier said than done.

Before concluding this chapter, I want to pay tribute to a colleague in medicine who succumbed to complications from COVID-19. Richard P. Mills, MD, MPH, embodied the cause of the common good. He was a leader in ophthalmology and carried the torch of volunteerism passed to him by a friend who founded EyeCare America in 1985. This charity is part of the Foundation of the American Academy of Ophthalmology, which has provided eye exams and treatment to the uninsured at no cost for over 35 years. The following obituary is taken from the Academy website.[57]

"For more than 3 decades, Dr. Mills was an integral part of Academy leadership, most notably as *EyeNet Magazine* chief medical editor, EyeCare America chair and Academy president. His 14 years of *EyeNet* columns were legendary, with a total of 148 opinion pieces that combined medicine, music, philosophy, lexicography and mythology with pop culture references—all the while shedding light on important issues facing ophthalmology. He was the honoree of the Foundation's Orbital Gala in 2016."

"Academy CEO David W. Parke II, MD, referred to Dr. Mills' contributions to the Academy as protean. 'He believed fervently that every ophthalmologist had a responsibility to serve others, rather than (as he referred to it) 'hitchhike' on the contributions of others,' said Dr. Parke. 'His laugh was unmistakable, and his comments were pithy and humorous. Dick was one of the good guys—the best guys. We will miss him."

I went back to read his editorial about hitchhiking on the professional road. His effective, witty shaming of those members of the Academy unconnected to State ophthalmological societies hit the mark. Our State ophthalmological societies function at the ground level, advocating for patient safety and for putting the volunteer in volunteerism.

We need to take care of each other, now more than ever.

Chapter 7

Family History

IN TAKING A CAREFUL FAMILY HISTORY during an encounter with a patient, a doctor asks questions about parents, siblings, children and relatives whose health status may bear upon the patient being examined. As in the prior chapter on Social History, the interconnectedness of factors relating to American institutions in general, and to health-care in particular, play an important role in looking for sources of distrust. A recent article[58] by Gerald F. Seib, a political reporter for the *Wall Street Journal,* captured the lack of trust experienced by millennials, the group currently between the ages of 18 and 34. This generation paid a high price for college tuition, incurred a great deal of debt, graduated and then experienced the economic contraction from the terrorist attacks of 9/11 and the financial crisis of 2008. Now this well-educated age group is the one most likely to lose a job as a result of the coronavirus pandemic. They could be excused for having such a pessimistic outlook, given what they have been through thus far. These traumatic economic events have colored their thinking, as evidenced by a representative for a progressive group of young people. "Anxiety caused by all these crises manifests itself in a belief that leaders can't really ever be trusted—that it's gotta be us that makes a change." He adds: "That means no one is looking for a singular leader to fix it. We don't need a hero."

Jaded is the word to describe some of the thinking about what it takes to succeed in a world where the deck is stacked against them. The following passage is taken from *Trick Mirror*.[59]

"Amazon, Uber and Airbnb are all cut from the same cloth. These companies represent a socially approved version of millennial scamming: the dream of being a 'founder' who gets a dumb idea, raises a ton of money, and sells the company before he has to do too much work." As if the founders of these companies did little work to earn their success.

I have a different mindset when it comes to notions of success. Hard work is the key ingredient, no matter what the circumstances. Yes, some may have certain economic advantages to begin their careers, but, in my opinion, success requires a determination to play the hand you are dealt in the best way possible to achieve your goals. Grit is something I respect, as evidenced by the following episode from a patient encounter just before I retired from medical practice.

Aspiring Writers

"So how's your writing going?" I asked my patient at her final visit with me. I had seen her six months previously for a chronic eye problem, and I wanted a last chance to assess her condition and say goodbye. I had learned of Becky's interest in writing at our last visit, when I'd announced my intention to retire in January 2019. A former high school teacher, Becky was a petite, elderly, intelligent woman with a mild head tremor. She asked me to hold her head still while I examined her at the slit lamp— she wanted to be sure that I had the best possible view of her eyes. I had successfully operated on her cataracts years ago despite her head tremor, and I had recently been treating her dry eye condition. We shared a common purpose in writing our memoirs, and my question to Becky opened up the floodgates.

"I have ten stories that are nearly complete. My goal is to describe some of the people who have positively influenced my life," Becky reported.

"So, you're approaching the final draft?"

"You might say so, but I hit a snag when the wife of a recently deceased gentleman complained that I had revealed too much of their private life. I wanted to get her opinion of my writing, but she felt it was just too personal. I need to go back and rework that particular vignette." Becky's smile showed her confidence.

"At my writing course, we were advised to avoid initials, proper names or references that could identify the people we write about. Sometimes we can use our memories to create composite characters that will have nearly the same impact." I was drawing on my own experience from the Harvard Writers' Course I had taken recently. Becky nodded her agreement.

"I plan to use fictitious names. It's hard not to mix autobiography with memoir. I grew up on lower Spruce Street in Manchester. My family was poor, we had nothing. My father was an alcoholic and never worked a day since the time I could remember. My mother worked hard to support us, four kids within three years of each other. She told me to take business courses in school to prepare me for a good job. I remember when a friend of the family brought my mother an olive green Army blanket. My mother smiled, said 'Becky needs a new winter coat.' She proceeded to dye the Army material, cut the pattern and sew the sleeves and hood. I was dubious at first that she could turn an Army blanket into a coat, but she did."

"What did you do with your business courses?"

"I was fortunate to land a secretarial job for a high school principal who later was promoted to superintendent, and I got promoted with him. He was demanding with the staff, and I did everything I could to complete my work on time and not make waves. I was a goodie-goodie, you could say. One day he asked me to come to his office, something he rarely did except to fire people. I asked my coworkers if I had done anything that could be construed as a firing offense, and they were as confused as I was. I entered his office at the appointed time, and he closed both doors. I was nearly in tears, expecting the worst. He cleared his throat and said, 'You don't belong in this office.' That did it for me. I knew I was fired. Instead, he said, 'You are a bright girl. There are just two careers for women, nursing and teaching. I suggest that you become a teacher.' I was shocked."

I had heard similar stories from other women about the limited opportunities that existed in that era, particularly once World War II ended. Some were told that only single women would be allowed to stay on the job. According to the logic at the time, once a woman married, her lot in life was secure, so the available jobs would go to the unmarried women who had to earn a living for themselves. I asked Becky to continue her story.

"My boss got up from the desk and went to a drawer and pulled out a huge key ring that held keys to all the schools. He pulled one off and handed it to me, saying 'this opens the front door to Central High School and the library. Use it to study when you can't find a quiet place at home. You're going to Notre Dame College in Manchester to get a teaching degree, and I am going to make sure that happens. No one deserves a scholarship more than you.' I couldn't believe it! I was going to become an educated professional!"

"He opened doors for you, no pun intended." I smiled as Becky recounted her memories. She told me that she had saved enough money from her secretarial job to cover her first year of college tuition. Her early life was a struggle, but she managed to expand her universe through persistence and hard work. I didn't break the spell by glancing at my watch, even though I knew I was late for my next appointment.

"I became a teacher, and in my class I had the cousin of the doctor you referred me to. He became a prominent attorney in Manchester. I was asked to return to the 50th class reunion for Central High, the class of 1968. It was wonderful to be recognized and thanked for helping my students on their career paths."

"You have much to be proud of, Becky. You represent what grit and drive can accomplish. I had my parents' support, emotional and financial, on my way to becoming a doctor, so I enjoyed advantages you never did. I admire you for what you've done with your life." I smiled, thinking how this woman was tough as nails but still had a giving heart.

"I established a foundation that awards a college scholarship. The criteria I chose was that the student had to be hard working and poor, like I was. The student should be smart, so I added that he or she should have completed calculus. What do you think?"

"I'm not the one to ask, Becky. I took calculus in high school in an accelerated program and managed a 'B' but I didn't really understand it. As a college freshman, I repeated calculus as a requirement for my pre-med courses, and I finally got it. Better late than never."

"I know you have to go, Doctor, but I want to thank you for listening to me. And thank you for all you've done to keep me seeing well. I am forever grateful."

"Becky, it has been a privilege to be your doctor. Keep up the good work with your eye drops—and your writing. I'll be anxious to read the final version of your memoir."

We shared a mutually encouraging hug, allowing patient and doctor, now two budding writers, a satisfying moment of affection and hope.

As we look at the devastation caused by the coronavirus, we should step back to get the big picture, to think more carefully about where we go from here. We must keep in perspective how we, as Americans, have responded to crises in the past. There is a can-do spirit that moves among us, even in the bleakest of conditions. And from an historical and evolutionary perspective, survival is in our genes, literally. An article[60] from Edwin Leap, MD, an emergency physician, was posted on KevinMD April 1, 2020, entitled, *In these dark times of a pandemic look to history for hope.*" Dr. Leap's message of hope builds upon our human history of successfully surmounting life-threatening obstacles.

"Go back far enough, and those who came before were regularly preyed upon by large animals. And yet, those who read this had ancestors who managed to evade those beasts. Others faced earthquakes, volcanic eruptions, ice ages, diseases, famine, dangerous childbirth, and tribal warfare. The full catalog of their suffering is lost to us. And yet their DNA remains; their '"children" live on today." Coming from an emergency physician on the front lines of the coronavirus attack, his words have special meaning.

"The coronavirus is certainly dangerous. Physicians and others who have spent years caring about dangerous infectious diseases are admittedly a bit unnerved."

"However, humanity will get through this. The coronavirus' mortality rate lags far behind the infectious nightmares that human ancestors passed through, especially since medications, vaccines, and equipment can be mass-produced, food is widely available, and information can be disseminated in an instant."

"Therefore if history is any indication or vindication, if the past is any lens for the future, this is still a time of tremendous hope. Especially for people, all people alive today, whose resilient ancestors survive through them to this very day."

We must trust our survival instincts. To get beyond this mess, we must also evaluate and apply guidelines[61] to protect those most vulnerable to infection by the coronavirus. We all have a part to play in this medical drama, regardless of the generation to which we belong.

Chapter 8

Review of Systems

"MEDICINE BEGINS WITH STORIES. Patients tell stories to describe illness; doctors tell stories to understand it. Science tells its story to explain diseases." The words of Siddhartha Mukherjee, MD, jumped off the page. Yes! I said to myself as I gathered my notes for this chapter, having read the remarkable book by the oncologist/hematologist, *The Emperor of All Maladies*.[62] In his Pulitzer Prize–winning book on the biology of cancer, the author describes the story of medicine, from earliest attempts to conquer diseases by bloodletting to modern use of genetic decoding to attack various conditions that threaten our lives. At some point in the development of drugs to combat different types of leukemia, doctors had to find the right balance of poisons to kill the tumor-producing cells without killing the host.[63] "These were the daredevils of medical research, acrobats devising new drugs that nearly killed patients; these men played chicken with death." However, the best clinicians are not just fighting a disease; they are fully engaged with their patients. In one episode from his fellowship training, Mukherjee follows an attending into the hospital room of his patient, a woman he called Fitz, knowing that the results of the tests did not favor survival.[64]

"Resuscitation," he called it cryptically as he strode into her room. I watched him resuscitate. He emphasized process over outcome and transmitted astonishing amounts of information with a touch so slight that you might not even feel it. He told Fitz about the tumor, the good news about the surgery, asked about her family, then spoke about his own. He spoke about his child who was complaining about her long days at school. Did Fitz have a grandchild? he inquired. Did a daughter or a son live close by? And then, as I watched, he began to insert numbers here and there with a light-handedness that was a marvel to observe."

If asked, patients will tell you if they sense a connection with their doctors. When trust is established, physicians may share details of their own lives with their patients, without compromising their professionalism. Showing patients that you understand their concerns demonstrates your humanity as a physician. That is particularly true in dealing with terminal illness; hope is the one consistent yearning of all such patients. The following poem was handed to a late friend of mine who had undergone extensive chemotherapy and radiation for prostate cancer as he left a post-treatment program at MD Anderson Cancer Center.

Lend me your hope for a while.
    I seem to have mislaid mine.
Loss and hopeless feelings accompany me daily.
    Pain and confusion are my companions.
I know not where to turn; looking ahead to future
    times does not bring forth images of renewed
    hope.
I see troubled times, pain-filled days, and more
    tragedy.

Lend me your hope for a while. I seem to have
    mislaid mine. Hold my hand and hug me; listen
    to all my ramblings, recovery seems so far
    distant. The road to healing seems like a long
    and lonely one.
Lend me your hope for a while. I seem to have
    mislaid mine. Stand by me. Offer me your
    presence, your heart and your love. Acknowl-
    edge my pain, it is so real and ever present.
    I am overwhelmed with sad and conflicting
    thoughts.
Lend me your hope for a while; a time will come
    when I heal, and I will share my renewal, hope
    and love with you and others.

When we are confronted with illness, we want our healers to address our psychological, as well as our physical,
needs. Doctors who can provide skill with compassion are
most appreciated. The question becomes, living within any
healthcare system, what are the odds that an individual
patient's needs can best be satisfied?

You don't have to look too far back in American history
to see the roots of our current healthcare system. When
the federal government froze wages for workers during
World War II, employers offered healthcare benefits to
their workers as a perk to stay on the job. The cost of such
health insurance was borne by the employer, and the
employee was not taxed on the benefit. While employer-
sponsored healthcare benefits grew, the administration
thereof developed as an industry of its own. Today, America's health plans have become a major economic force.

Their business model was originally designed to cover workers and their families, but plans were extended to individuals and underwritten according to demographic criteria, including age, sex, and habits such as smoking.

Having a "J" Plan from Blue Cross Blue Shield was considered the gold standard for coverage when I entered medical practice in the early 1980s. It covered most types of care for conditions treated either in the office of the doctor or in the hospital. Such an extensive array of health benefits provided a sense of confidence that if things went wrong, patients did not pay out-of-pocket for care. However, as the cost of these plans continued to increase, employers were challenged to find a formula that would allow some participation by the employee for cost-sharing or would limit the total payout of benefits. Such plans were "capped" so that in the course of a serious illness, such as needing heart surgery for example, patients would get stuck with the balance that was not paid by their plan. Furthermore, plans were allowed by law to discriminate on the basis of pre-existing health conditions that would either exclude individuals from insurance completely or charge them much higher premiums. Insurance companies held all the cards, and they determined the rules of the game.

Contributing to distrust of insurance companies was their policy of squeezing cost savings through expedited hospital discharges. Health insurance plans, and hospitals dependent on their payments, earned a reputation for predatory behavior, captured in the phrase "drive-through deliveries" for maternal care. It took an act of Congress to extend the insurance plans' coverage for, and hospitals' practice of, only 24 hours of care for new mothers. People were getting really annoyed. The presidential election of 1992 reflected, in part, the importance of healthcare and the need to do something about changing the system.

When the Clintons entered the White House, Bill had tasked Hillary with coming up with a better healthcare system. I traveled to Hanover, New Hampshire, to hear the First Lady's speech to the medical community about how the US government was going to alter the balance of power among the players in the healthcare system. Her task force, composed of academics, think-tank experts and social scientists, would alter the face of medicine through cooperatives supported by the federal government. "Hillarycare" was the first among the moniker-branded cares with a broad vision for changing the healthcare system. While some doctors embraced the concept emphasizing primary care and preventive care, others, particularly medical and surgical specialists, felt that they had been excluded from the early planning phase of the proposal. The legislative momentum driven by Hillary Clinton was effectively gutted by an aggressive advertising campaign created to show how the "common man" got screwed under the proposal. Harry and Louise, characters featured in the now famous TV commercials, conducted their own focus group as a couple at the dinner table, citing the horrors of a government-run healthcare system. The message was clear: Hillarycare meant the end of private health insurance. The group behind the ads was, of course, composed of those with the most to lose by changing the system— health insurance companies. What the ads did was sow distrust in an enterprise that had been conceived largely in secret. The bill, constructed as a top-down policy lacking significant input from doctors working "in the trenches," never made it to the President's desk.

Fast forward to the election of Barack Obama in 2008. With a single political party controlling both chambers of Congress and the Presidency, the progressive agenda to restructure our healthcare system was given new life. What developed from multiple committees in both the House and Senate, with some unsubtle nudging by the President's economic advisors, was the chaotic process of drafting legislation to favor diverse constituencies. The chairs of the Congressional committees in all cases were Democrats with reputations earned for promoting progressive policies for healthcare and financial matters. Steven Brill's book, *America's Bitter Pill: Money, Politics, Backroom Deals, and the Fight to Fix Our Broken Healthcare System*[65] is an encyclopedic account of how "Obamacare" was constructed. The Big Players in healthcare—health insurance companies, pharmaceutical companies, pharmacy benefits managers, medical device manufacturers, the hospital association and physician groups—confronted, with a major lobbying effort, the prospects of a complex system designed to provide care for the uninsured. The bill was cloaked in "revenue neutral" terms as far as the federal budget was concerned, clearly a fiction even before the bill was passed. The promised "doc fix" (to correct a law that threatened physicians' federal payments year after year) was eliminated from the final draft of the bill because of budget constraints. The Obama Administration's commitment to the American Medical Association, which had endorsed the Patient Protection and Affordable Care Act in the early days of the legislative draft, was put off for another year.

The consequences of that decision to rescind a promise would be minimal, according to the President's advisors.[66]

"The decision to drop the "doc fix" from the bill was emblematic of two important dynamics. First, the doctors—the players in the healthcare economy who, with nurses, actually provide healthcare—had seen their influence evaporate compared to the big-money industry stakeholders such as the drug companies, insurers, and hospitals. As a result, they could be trifled with in a way that would have been unimaginable in the Truman era, when they had almost single-handedly torpedoed reform. They just didn't have that clout anymore...Second, the doc fix gambit (deferral to another bill at a later time) made it clear that the Congressional Budget Office scoring process was more a game to be played than it was a precise measuring device to be read like a thermometer."

In retrospect, the comments made by the President to a gathering of the American Medical Association[67] would prove to be false. Once the law was passed, mandated benefits for all policies sold in the US caused premiums to skyrocket. Provider networks were shrunken to allow insurance companies to recoup losses, resulting in patients losing their physicians of choice. Furthermore, some patients had their current health insurance policies cancelled because these policies didn't conform to the "standard benefits" all plans were required to include.

"Obama took to the stump, telling an American Medical Association convention that "we will keep this promise to the American people: If you like your doctor, you will be able to keep your doctor, period. If you like your health care plan, you'll be able to keep your health care plan, period. No one will take it away, no matter what."

After reading Brill's account, it is hard to come away with anything but distrust in the creation of the "Frankenstein" that was to become the law of the land, affecting one-sixth of America's economy. Brill's reporting was spot on, but he couldn't resist some editorial comment. By the conclusion of this non-fiction work, his own personal medical nightmare had faded; the best cardiothoracic surgeon around had already fixed his aneurysm. When viewed from the pre-op stretcher, the mind wants only the best healthcare, no matter the cost. What Brill proposes is a transition to a healthcare system modeled on the robber barons of the American industrial age. The difference, compared with the former age of monopolies in terms of competition for insured patients, would result from a few oligopolies created from medical centers merging with insurance companies. Such healthcare Goliaths would be regulated for their prices and profits, much as rates for public utilities are regulated. In Brill's ideal world of healthcare, all physicians become employees of these giant merged entities. By his logic, the interests of patients, physicians and administrators are blissfully aligned with the interests of the CEOs of the new megacenters whose salaries are dictated by a commission established by, you might have guessed, the federal government. Controlling the means of production, in this case the delivery of healthcare, has always been a socialist ideal, even if the reality is less than desirable. Before he left office, President Obama penned a Special Communication to the *Journal of the American Medical Association*, touting the benefits of his signature legislative accomplishment.[68]

Under the *Conclusions and Relevance* section of this JAMA article, Obama wrote "Policymakers should build on progress made by the Affordable Care Act by continuing to implement the Health Insurance Marketplaces and delivery system reform, increasing federal financial assistance for Marketplace enrollees, introducing a public plan option in areas lacking individual market competition, and taking actions to reduce prescription drug costs. Although partisanship and special interest opposition remain, experience with the Affordable Care Act demonstrates that positive change is achievable on some of the nation's most complex challenges."

Not everyone agrees with his conclusions. As far as Obama's suggestion goes for a public option to restructure healthcare, the next election will likely decide what form, if any, a public option will assume. Given the challenges presented by the coronavirus in 2020, the importance of healthcare in a national election will once again find itself near the top of the electorate's concerns. And not surprisingly, the partisans the former President referred to are launching their own ideas for healthcare reform, based on market principles.

In her book[69], *False Premise, False Promise: The Disastrous Reality of Medicare for All*, Sally C. Pipes argues that assuming healthcare is a right, rather than a commodity with limited resources, is a false assumption. The false promise is that "free care" can be given to every American and that the federal government should foot the bill. In his foreword to the book, the late US Senator Tom Coburn, MD, writes that the author knows something about nationalized healthcare, having lived in Canada and studied the United Kingdom National Health Service. Her account of care rationing and of delays in treatment is unsettling for anyone with an open mind. Some of Pipe's recommendations for reform include making health savings accounts (HSAs) available to everyone, not just those with high-deductible insurance plans. She would expand HSAs to allow Medicare subscribers to pay premiums, rather than deducting the cost of premiums from Social Security, as the current law requires. Pipes targets costs by embracing telemedicine, a feature of patient engagement greatly expanded during the COVID lockdowns, to reduce unnecessary trips to the emergency room. She would resurrect tort reform, a feature that was originally part of the agreement between organized medicine and the Obama Administration in drafting the ACA, but that had been ultimately relegated to demonstration status and never funded in the final bill. Defensive medicine adds unnecessary cost to the healthcare system. Therefore, non-economic damages sought by attorneys from physicians' malpractice insurance carriers in negligence suits would be capped. To better protect health insurance subscribers and to lower costs, Pipes challenges the companies issuing the policies.[70]

"Insurers should be required to cover anyone who maintains continuous coverage from year to year, without raising their premiums if they get sick. A continuous coverage requirement will incentivize young and healthy people to buy and hold insurance, since they'll want to lock in lower premiums while they can. That will ensure a steady flow of premiums into the insurance risk pool and prevent the unintended spike in cost that occurs when people only sign up for coverage after getting sick." As part of doing business in health insurance, companies would be required to share in risk pools for those with preexisting conditions that tend to bump up the cost of care for all subscribers.

Not all of the recommendations offered by Pipes will see the legislative light of day. Taxing the value of employer-sponsored healthcare benefits, as the Obamacare "Cadillac tax" intended to do, negates the hard-fought benefits achieved by unions in collective bargaining with employers. The position taken by the late Senator John McCain in the 2008 presidential election campaign to tax such benefits as a way of subsidizing the uninsured was a non-starter. It is not a popular idea to mess with employer-sponsored health-care benefits. In order to put the brakes on Medicare spending, Pipes proposes vouchers for seniors, a subject Congressman Paul Ryan had unsuccessfully introduced while then Speaker of the House. Furthermore, her recommendation to expand state scope of practice laws for limited-license healthcare providers introduces again the problem of cutting corners for quality care (see Chapter 5).

Policy considerations need to be tested, in my opinion, by the litmus test of benefit to patients. If a policy compromises the patient-doctor relationship, it should be modified or discarded. Parties impacting the patient-physician relationship in healthcare policy currently have extraordinary reserves of money for lobbying purposes.

TOTAL DOLLARS SPENT IN 2019 ON LOBBYING BY NOTABLE HEALTH ORGANIZATIONS	
Organization	**USD (millions)**
Pharmaceutical Research and Manufacturers of America	29.29
American Hospital Association	26.22
Blue Cross/Blue Shield	25.15
American Medical Association	20.91
America's Health Insurance Plans	9.54

What astounds me is that the total spending on health sector lobbying through January 2020 approached $600,000,000, according to the Center for Responsive Politics, a non-partisan, non-profit organization.[71] I suppose I should not be surprised; 2020 is an election year, and the stakes are high for industries targeted by healthcare reformers.

Just how big are the Big Players in healthcare? The K Street lobbyists have become extremely efficient in managing the policymakers in Congress. Dr. Elaina George's book illustrates how "middlemen" to the patient-doctor relationship have highjacked healthcare.[72]

"Without competition among different hospital systems—or between formerly independent physician specialty groups—the price of medical services will likely increase. The large hospital systems have clearly pursued a strategy to organize themselves into non-competing systems which are the only game in town, removing any choice for the patient. When you add to the fact that they have begun to offer their own hospital based insurance which locks patients into their hospital network because they won't cover out of network benefits, it is clear that they have become nothing more than medical cartels."

Dr. George is a practicing ear, nose and throat specialist who decided that she would no longer play the game forced upon her by the Big Players. She has established a practice of direct patient care for which she does not accept insurance. Not every doctor can take that financial risk and remain in private practice. However, every doctor should stand for patients as the reform wave continues to pound our shore as professionals. She is an advocate for patients and physicians.[73]

"As physicians, we take an oath to do no harm. Sometimes it seems that after taking the Hippocratic Oath, we take another oath—to keep quiet. Physicians have to understand that healthcare is now subject to elective politics and advocacy by interest groups. This means that for the sake of our patients, we have to speak out. We are respected in our communities; people will listen to us if we can communicate our advocacy for patients. One of the greatest harms we do is to remain quiet. Physicians need to explain what is happening to their patients, and together, they must make their voices heard before individual choices are legislated away."

On the March 30, 2020, podcast from *Rx for Success*, the guest physician was Marion Mass, MD, a physician advocate and practicing pediatrician. Her primary topic for discussion[74] was kickbacks allowed under the safe harbor provisions of the US Stark Laws for Group Purchasing Organizations and for Pharmacy Benefits Managers (PBMs). These Big Players derive great financial benefit from markups on the purchase of hospital supplies and on wholesale pharmaceutical sales to pharmacies, respectively. The industry has undergone consolidation with only a few companies controlling 80% of the market. It has become so lucrative that the affiliated PBMs have acquired large health plans worth billions of dollars. Middlemen have found a niche in healthcare purchasing, and they have pressed their advantage in the market. One example is CVS Health acquiring Aetna in 2018 for $70 billion. It is the stated goal of the CEO of the merged entity to broaden the service portfolio of the affiliated pharmacies, allowing pharmacists to host "minute clinics" staffed by nurse practitioners for walk-in primary care. Convenience should not trump quality, and it remains to be seen whether this business plan will succeed as intended with the general public.

A recent study by the Rand Corporation looked at various healthcare reform proposals related to the Affordable Care Act to answer the question, "Revise or Replace?" The conclusions drawn by the author of the study, Christine Eibner, set the stage for the healthcare debates in an election year.[75]

"As policymakers weigh the choices ahead, it is clear that tensions exist between many health policy goals—for example, expanding coverage versus reducing costs; targeting tax credits effectively versus incentivizing work; protecting the sickest and most expensive patients versus preserving choice among the majority of patients who may not need comprehensive coverage; and limiting the federal government's cost liability versus minimizing cost-shifting to consumers and states. Deciding among these goals or striking a balance across them will involve political and value calculations about what the U.S. health care system should look like."

Spoiler alert: The ACA will not go away. As of this writing, the US Supreme Court has ruled 8-1 in favor of plaintiffs over claims for reimbursement for "risk corridors." The federal government agreed to assume the risk for insurance companies that may have expenses in excess of revenue as participants in the Obamacare exchanges. Congress reneged in funding the risk corridors, and the Court found in favor of the insurance company plaintiffs. When the law was passed in its original form, the deal made between the health insurance companies and the Obama Administration created a mechanism to off-load financial risk. The provision for risk corridors would cover costs in excess of premiums paid in by new subscribers created by the law. As most observers would assume, with so many previously uninsured chronically ill people now eligible for health insurance through the exchanges, insurance companies took a financial hit on the arrangement. Some cooperatives established as non-profits to participate in the exchanges went out of business because the funds to make up the losses never arrived. Congress voted not to fund the risk corridors after the law was passed, and the defendants in the lawsuit simply said, "too bad." The Supreme Court had a different interpretation. It found in favor of the plaintiffs, the insurance companies who had agreed to the implied contract. In consideration for participating in the new exchanges, the companies would receive protection by the federal government via the risk corridors. Per the Court decision, any damages for not funding the corridors would be distributed among the companies party to the lawsuit by a formula yet to be determined. The Big Players in the health insurance game wrote off the losses before the Court decision because they had the cash reserves to do so. The smaller companies, those unlucky non-profits that went bankrupt before the suit could be won, were simply forgotten. Trust in government has its price.

Why is this ACA-related Supreme Court decision important? The analogy can be made to the white smoke emanating from The Vatican when a major decision is made, namely the selection of the next Pope. This court

decision sets the stage for a decision to reaffirm the constitutionality of Obamacare. Chief Justice Roberts gave his
landmark majority opinion in the 5-4 decision to uphold
the constitutionality of the original law when the mandate
to obtain insurance coverage was, in his opinion, a tax that
could be levied by Congress. His legal argument was
assailed by critics, particularly since the law carefully
avoided the term "tax" because of its negative connotation
by the public. Whatever you want to call it—a tax, an obli-
gation or a requirement by law to pay a fine by not acting
accordingly—the Chief Justice reasoned that it would stand.
In his brief, the Chief Justice also implied that if Congress
had intended to tax Americans, it should have stated as
much. For the sake of the newly insured subscribers under
Obamacare, the Court held that the law was constitutional.
A similar conclusion, I would expect, should come after
the 2020 national election when the Court takes up another
wrinkle on the question of the constitutionality of the ACA.

Arguments to the Court have been made that the law
is invalid, now that the mandate for coverage has been
effectively removed. The cost for not having health insurance was reduced to zero by the Republican-controlled
Congress as a provision of the Tax Reform Act of 2017.
According to the plaintiffs, by eliminating the "tax" for not
obtaining insurance coverage (arguably the requirement
that binds the entire benefit structure of Obamacare), the
law is now unconstitutional. In my humble non-legal opinion, I believe that a thin majority of the Court will once
again uphold the law. The winning argument, after all of
the scholarly back and forth, will be that ten years after
the law's passage, just too many people depend on it for

access to health insurance to throw the law out.

What do surveys tell us about the issue of healthcare in the upcoming election? The majority of respondents believe that Obamacare should be modified, not discarded. People have been hit hard by high deductibles and co-pays for any insurance product,[76] and they are seeking solutions. The Bipartisan Policy Center, in its January 2020 survey, offered the following conclusion.[77]

"Of the heath care reforms tested, improving the current health care system, rather than repealing and replacing the ACA or Medicare-for-All, receives the most bipartisan support." The coronavirus pandemic may alter the terms of the debate over what shape healthcare reform will take in the future, but one thing appears certain: our views of healthcare and those who provide it will never be the same.

The metamorphosis of healthcare delivery is happening right before our eyes. Will we become a society in which patient-centered care is replaced by artificial intelligence–driven algorithms, supported by oligopolies of mega medical centers providing their own brand of health insurance and funded by high-priced drugs? Will our healthcare fall victim to universal coverage scripted by government officials? As the political humorist P.J. O'Rourke has quipped, "If you think healthcare is expensive now, wait until you see the cost when it's free." Or will some other system evolve that respects the bond between patient and doctor while reducing cost and ensuring quality? My prescription for rebuilding trust in healthcare intends to do just that. But first, I have to perform a Physical Exam and report my findings to our hypothetical panel of medical experts on why distrust has become so pervasive.

Chapter 9

Physical Exam

IT WAS 2019, the year I chose to retire from medicine. Little did I know just how much the world of medicine would change with the emergence of COVID-19. However, 2019 was also the year when an important book was published on the status of the US healthcare system from a *New York Times* best-selling author. In his acclaimed book, *The Price We Pay: What Broke American Health Care—And How to Fix It*, Marty Makary, MD, traces the growth of the medical industrial complex and how individual patients have been taken advantage of by the system.[78] Dr. Makary's thesis relates to the lack of transparency in pricing for medical services. A cancer surgeon who also teaches at the Johns Hopkins Bloomberg School of Health, Dr. Makary has traveled extensively across America to study and to report on the ways in which the healthcare system has gotten out of control. Unfortunately for the individual patient, with or without health insurance, the deck is stacked against receiving fair service at a fair price.

Fair, compared to what, you might be thinking. That's his point; you have no means by which to compare service, quality or price because the formulas that shoppers normally use for making decisions are simply unavailable to most people when needing healthcare. There are no price tags attached to the most expensive services. The crunch for cash is particularly felt when someone must seek emergency care. Some hospital systems had hired a team of bill collectors, dressed them in white coats, handed them clip-boards with a place for patients' credit card numbers, and released them to the emergency department. Upon admission, insured patients were confronted by the bill collectors to pay up front for their co-pay or deductible. A smiling "staff member" for a company specializing in such pressure tactics usually collected the money, because the patient was frightened and confused at the time. This highly unethical process was eventually outlawed—but not before such companies thrived from the commissions paid by the hospital administration. Those without insurance, or living in poverty, were subjected to enormous bills generated by the hospitals' "chargemaster," an inflated bill that shocked those receiving it. Some CEOs of hospitals attempted to deflect criticism of going after patients for partial payment or non-payment, suggesting that the bill was actually a first bid in the negotiation process. These hospital executives offered payment plans on exorbitant bills, as if that were a concession rather than the law. When Dr. Makary appeared in court as an expert witness on cases for such financially abused patients, the hospital withdrew the civil suits for garnishing wages. According to Makary, the business plan for hospitals, which themselves suffered price gouging at the hands of their Group Purchasing Organizations, had evolved to mimic that of a payday lender.

Why should patients be forced to negotiate in the first place? For the 60% of medical care that is "shoppable" according to Makary, price transparency would put the consumer of care in a more powerful position—having the knowledge of what he or she would pay *ahead of time*. That concept of consumer knowledge was used in a program established in Utah to estimate the out-of-pocket expenses for elective procedures, based on the insurance product the subscriber had. Plug in your health insurance carrier, your personal information for the plan you had, and, voila! you were sent an estimate. That process was acceptable to most people who used the service, but it did not really address the transparency issue. Private, commercial insurance would always pay more than government-supported insurance (Medicare and Medicaid). The hospital did not have to reveal the terms by which it did business with the insurance company. In fact, as part of a contract for a broad level of services offered by a large panel of participating physicians, the hospital had to sign a non-disclosure agreement with the insurance company preventing them from revealing the outcome of negotiated fees. Dr. Makary cites brokenhealthcare.org as a source for further information on how price transparency can help individual patients swim with the sharks without getting eaten.

A section in Dr. Makary's book resonates with me when it comes to medical education and what we, as patients, want from our doctors.[79] I excerpt here from the text because the author says what I am thinking better than I could. He refers to a physician-CEO of an institution for medical education who emphasizes empathy and communication as key elements in developing the clinical skills doctors require.

"Unfortunately, most medical schools still haze students by making them commit to memory thousands of details that do not need to be rapidly recalled in the real world of doctoring. Some medical schools blame the accrediting boards for requiring all the memorization. Well, here's an open invitation to the old guard of medical school accreditation: come spend a day with me in the hospital..."

"Medical schools should take a lesson from the innovators in medical education today, like Dr. Stephen Klasko, CEO of Thomas Jefferson University and Jefferson Health. Dr. Klasko is restructuring medical education to teach humility and compassion...Klasko believes in making medical education highly relevant to the medical, social and financial needs of patients—the whole person."

"He learned that the way we select and educate physicians is akin to joining a cult. He identified four fundamental traits that get ingrained early: a competitive bias, an autonomy bias, a hierarchy bias, and a noncreativity bias."

"Under Klasko's leadership, Jefferson selects students based on their emotional intelligence and trains them to be highly effective communicators with sound clinical judgment."

"People like Klasko are changing the culture of medicine for the better by putting the focus back on the patient."

As patients, we need compassion and communication with caregivers the most when facing uncertainty. In no other time in living memory have we been challenged, as patients and as doctors, as we have with the coronavirus pandemic. The lead up to, and the immersion in, the trials and tribulations patients and doctors faced as COVID-19 hit our shores, amount to a multi-month nightmare. It presented as a comedy of errors but no laughing matter. Ignored were the warnings of potential pandemics by the likes of Bill and Melinda Gates, whose foundation had worked to combat outbreaks of Ebola virus in Africa. Companies originally contracted by the federal government to make inexpensive respirators had been acquired by larger fish, and the contract provisions that had been negotiated were eliminated in the merger.[80] The failure to follow recommendations of the public health officials in New York, compared with Seattle, allowed for greater spread of the virus.[81] Poor communication in the Trump Administration caused unnecessary delays in establishing a game plan to face the epidemic.[82] Front line healthcare workers, already stressed by the demands of the job, fell victim to the enormous human cost of this deadly enemy.[83] Cries from doctors treating the sickest patients echoed in social media.[84] The message was consistent; after this pandemic, nothing will ever be the same.[85]

One of the most familiar faces we saw on the President's Coronavirus Task Force was that of Anthony Fauci, MD. A lengthy article[86] in the *New Yorker* traced his career from his high school days through his efforts to combat HIV/AIDS and ultimately COVID-19. He had a way of blending caution with encouragement, safety with hope. He was reserved about making predictions for when treatments and vaccines would be available. He was criticized, as an infectious diseases expert, for his alleged myopic view of prevention of spread of disease at the expense of an economy barely on life support. The conflicts that arose from plans to open up the economy originated in part from the notion of risk versus reward. Yes, there is a health risk to allowing people to interact (within the confines of social distancing) in public places, but there is also financial risk for not allowing some return to business operations. My former eye care practice saw patients on an emergency basis only, rescheduling hundreds of elective surgical patients and keeping a skeleton crew working while furloughing many loyal employees. When over 80% of your business comes to a standstill, you have to get creative. The CARES Act helped many small businesses survive but not all were so fortunate.

I finally got a haircut, three months overdue, in May 2020. On my way to my barber of 25 years, I passed my favorite sandwich shop, the *Stuffed Sub* on Elm Street in Manchester, New Hampshire. The sign on the door made me sad, because the owner's announcement of a failed small business was duplicated by thousands of businesses, large and small.

"CLOSED PERMANENTLY!! Due to the unfortunate Virus Pandemic we have decided to close down permanently. Matt and Staff sincerely Thank You for 15 wonderful years of support and friendship! We will miss all of you! God Bless & please be safe!!"

As I look back on these unsettling events, I have come to the following conclusions. When we most needed reliable information, we received confused messaging. When we asked our frontline healthcare workers to face risk of infection, we did not give them access to appropriate protective gear. When physicians working in major hospitals called out their administrators for better ammunition to confront the virus, they were given gag orders.[87] The level of distrust in healthcare was palpable. It found expression in virtue signaling; if you cared, you wore a mask and if you didn't care, you didn't. If you wanted to open up the economy so that the people who work and need a paycheck could make ends meet, you were not serving the common good as you increased the risk of spread.

Ernie Johnson, a TV sports host, offered a moving account of his decision not to join the broadcast group for *The Match*, a charity golf match between Tiger Woods and Peyton Manning on one side, and Phil Mickelson and Tom Brady on the other. That event received $20 million in donations for COVID relief. But Johnson chose to stay away, citing his son who had taken every breath for the last nine years on a ventilator, a consequence of muscular dystrophy. The risk of bringing home an invisible invader was not worth it.[88] In some fashion, we have all made decisions based on risk and reward, and we must live with the consequences.

In sports, the consequence of playing a bad game may be a loss; with COVID-19, the consequence of infection may be loss of life. With such high stakes, our representatives in local, state and federal government have a lot of variables to weigh as the restrictions on personal interaction begin to ease. Our federalist system allows for autonomy of states, each characterized by its unique aspects of ethnic diversity, culture, administration of laws, taxing and setting priorities for its residents. Given such a heterogeneous collection of populations, one might expect diversity of response from governors, even if the incidence and severity of COVID were uniform across states. The great American experiment in reopening the economy is already up and running. In Professor McClay's book, *Land of Hope: An invitation to the Great American Story*,[89] the author describes how the tensions between states culminated in the Civil War and what lessons were learned in its aftermath. Our system of federal government is designed to deal with tensions among competing interests before war erupts. McClay may have to add an addendum to his book noting how divisions over reopening our economy have ultimately played out. Federal guidance issued for safely reopening businesses, schools, places of worship and recreational areas were followed according to the best data available to governors, but the final decision rested with these chief executives of the states. In the early days of the pandemic, we followed government rules and shut down the economy. The consciousness of a nation was focused on flattening the curve of new cases so as to not overwhelm capacity for intensive hospital care. Once that milestone was generally achieved, pressure to reopen was palpable. Political divisions that were already present rose up, reflecting the differences in attitude toward individual benefit versus the greater good of society.[90] Tough choices had to be made.[91]

What will our "new normal" look like as we emerge from near total shutdown? I believe that most people will adopt common sense approaches with greater hygiene, both personal and environmental. We will continue to develop better safeguards for our supply chain for protective equipment. We will see accelerated efforts by public and private sources for new drugs and vaccines. We know from the study of viruses that there will be another eruption in the future, whether caused by corona or another variant. Next time an eruption occurs, and it will, we better be prepared.

Chapter 10

Assessment and Plan

The Experts Speak on Zoom

I HAVE PRESENTED THE CASE for distrust in healthcare, and now it's time to bring in the experts to help with the Assessment and Plan to rebuild trust. Please note that the format I have chosen is purely fictional, a Zoom meeting I moderate. While the names of the panelists are fictional, the opinions expressed come from real people. The panelists include an array of distinguished doctors, educators and healthcare executives with strong feelings about the role of physicians and their relationship with patients. (Also note, I have chosen representative topics for the meeting to reflect categories that Kevin Pho, MD, uses for posting stories on KevinMD.com.) The format of experts presenting their opinions in a fictional Zoom meeting differs significantly from my personal narrative to this point. However, it will prove a useful device as the experts weigh in on what elements are essential for rebuilding trust. A tip from a former English teacher said to me, "Grant the author his or her material; criticize the way it is executed."

If you have ever attended a Zoom meeting, you understand the parameters for communication. Each participant must speak uninterrupted, or else the audio feed gets messed up among the computers connected for the meeting. Unlike a real meeting, such as grand rounds at a hospital where speakers can chime in when so moved, the Zoom format requires that each speaker offers a monologue and then fields questions later. A good moderator directs the program and personalizes the introductions to the presenters. At the end of the Zoom meeting, the moderator thanks the participants and offers a wrap up of significant ideas and suggests elements of consensus for going forward. It's my book and, to be expected, I get the last word!

The meeting is about to begin. Turn up the volume on your laptop computer and click on the online invitation sent to your email. Welcome to the meeting!

Good afternoon and welcome to this Zoom meeting on rebuilding trust in healthcare. I'm Dr. Paul Pender, your host for this event. With me on the panel is a distinguished group of individuals who share my passion for advocacy for patients and doctors. Before I introduce our first speaker, I would like to take care of some housekeeping items related to the organization of the meeting. Those who attend are in listen-only mode on their computers. The panelists will offer their individual assessments of the case I have presented, along with recommendations. Questions from the panel to the speaker are permitted, but these should be reserved for the end of the individual speaker's presentation to avoid the audio disruptions that arise from multiple voices speaking at the same time. Virtual attendees may submit questions to the panel from your computer. I have access to those questions and will edit as needed to keep the discussion moving. Once each member of the panel has spoken, using notes and graphs as required emphasizing their points, I will wrap up the session and offer some final thoughts.

Dr. Pender: I am pleased to introduce Dr. Patricia Patients, a geneticist teaching at a major university. Pat, you have the floor.

Dr. Patients: Thanks, Paul, for inviting me to the program. Zoom is a platform that has seen a lot of use lately! I am honored to be the lead speaker for this discussion about rebuilding trust in healthcare. The audience may wonder why a researcher in genetics should begin our program. I submit that individual consideration in structuring a workable solution to distrust in healthcare begins with fundamental concepts of our unique genetic blueprints. How can improvements in healthcare delivery be proposed that do not look to individual needs of patients? I have read the journal articles and books of Dr. Mukherjee mentioned earlier in your case presentation, Paul. A quote from his book, *The Emperor of All Maladies,* seems pertinent as we go about assessing the solutions required by individual patients. While his words speak to the use of chemotherapeutic agents, the same could be said about a "one size fits all" approach to healthcare.[92] "Systemic therapy without specificity is an indiscriminate bomb." I believe that patients deserve to be considered unique in their habits, culture, environment and all of the components that make us human. Physicians must be cognizant of these important elements influencing the health of their patients, just as a geneticist looks to individual base pairs in DNA to unlock the puzzle of our biology.

Dr. Pender: Thanks, Pat. You got us thinking right from the start. Perhaps our next speaker, Dr. Edward Edu, a clinical psychologist and award-winning author, would like to take it from here.

Dr. Edu: That's a perfect segue for me, Paul. My interests, both professional in the world of psychology and personal in what I seek in my physician, coincide with the subject of medical education. It is our responsibility to assist physicians in developing skills that help them achieve a balance between understanding scientific facts and the thoughts and emotions that make us human. If medical students are allowed to emerge from their competitive shells to acknowledge their fears, concerns and vulnerabilities, that is, to demonstrate their humanity, they will be better equipped to engage the vulnerabilities of their patients. One of the best presentations I have seen on the subject is a TED talk given by Laurel Braitman, an author and educator of the highest regard. The title of her talk is *The Mental Health Benefits of Storytelling for Healthcare Workers*.[93] Her students at Stanford Medical School find it therapeutic to write about their personal experiences, episodes from their lives that were kept hidden for fear of condemnation by their peers. The psychological benefit of narrative writing has been well established in the literature. As a formal exercise for medical students, Ms. Braitman concludes, "If this were a mental health drug, it would be an absolute blockbuster." She goes on to say, "this allows doctors and others an opportunity to envision a different kind of future for themselves and their patients." I will finish my remarks with a final quote from Ms. Braitman on why this approach to educating our healthcare workers is so important. "Helping healthcare professionals communicate more meaningfully with each other, with their patients and with themselves, is certainly not going to magically change everything that is wrong with the contemporary healthcare system, and it's not going to lift the immense burdens we place on our physicians, but it is absolutely key in making sure that our healers are healthy enough to heal the rest of us."

Dr. Pender: Thanks, Ed, that was terrific. Graduating competent, caring healthcare professionals is an important goal for society, but what can be said about our current crop of doctors? Let me introduce our next presenter, Dr. Peter Physicians, an authority on what doctors have experienced in their professional and personal lives following the onset of the coronavirus pandemic.

Dr. Physicians: Thanks for inviting me, Paul, and I will do my best to remain brief in my presentation. It's not easy, given the seismic impact of the virus on doctors and their responses. For professionals accustomed to regular routines in taking care of their patients—whether in the lab, the outpatient setting or in the hospital—doctors were forced to adapt to conditions and to extremes of severe illness they had rarely been exposed to in the past. Challenges to their sense of professionalism were expressed in burnout long before COVID-19.[94] One psychiatrist wrote on KevinMD that the next pandemic would be in mental health for patients and doctors alike.[95] Using the stages of grief from the model proposed by Elizabeth Kubler Ross—denial, anger, bargaining, depression and acceptance—Dr. Hamdani describes how we must work through this ordeal. Dr. Flora offered his insights on controlling what we can do and letting go of what we can't. His thought-provoking essay[96] was inspired by one of his oncology patients who told him, "When there is no wind, we row." Numerous articles in the lay press and on social media portrayed frontline healthcare workers as heroes. Some doctors and collaborators object to the term hero because they are simply doing the job that is expected of them.[97] Dr. Sarah Araji penned a post on KevinMD entitled, *It took a pandemic to reveal the secret of healthcare workers*.[98] I will conclude my presentation on rebuilding trust between patients and physicians with a quote from her essay.

"I know in this day and age access to health care has changed, technology and available resources online have sometimes created doubts and decreased trust in health care. I also know that some health care workers are seen as highly paid people (sometimes) that you can avoid seeing by just finding the answer online. But I hope this pandemic has brought back the confidence and trust in health care workers because at the end of the day there is nothing that can replace scientific facts given by someone who spent years studying and treating patients to be able to give optimal care."

Dr. Pender: I couldn't agree more, Peter. The coronavirus pandemic has focused the attention of everyone, not just physicians. Our next speaker is an expert on the epidemiology of COVID-19. Dr. Cary Conditions, the floor is yours.

Dr. Conditions: Thanks, Paul. It is hard not to speak in hyperbole when describing the extent of the damage caused by the coronavirus. Not only has it taken the lives of hundreds of thousands of people worldwide, it has shaken the confidence of our citizens in our healthcare system. It is a scourge without precedent in its rapidity of spread, thanks in part to a much more mobile world population than the one that existed at the time of the 1918 influenza pandemic. What we now know, as of spring 2020, is that anecdotal reports of benefit from oral hydroxychloroquine did not pan out in the studies reported to date. There is evidence that intravenous remdesivir, when given to critically ill hospital patients, seems to shorten the duration of COVID-19 and the length of hospital stay. We still don't know the best time to administer the treatment, and the results of studies are pending. We do not yet have a vaccine, but some promising results from early studies give us hope for combatting this plague.[99] A summary of all therapeutic bullets investigated as of April 2020 was published in the *Journal of the American Medical Association Network*.[100] Table 2 in the review article summarizes treatment and clinical outcomes from early COVID-19 clinical series. The slide I'm showing is busy, but right now we try to support the infected patient and to mute the cytokine storm that triggers multiple organ failure. There is some suggestion that convalescent plasma, derived from previously infected persons, may provide some benefit, but the jury is still out.

Dr. Pender: Thanks, Cary. We appreciate your insights. If the attendees have questions for the presenters, type them in the box on your computer screen and we will try to answer them at the end of the meeting. It is my pleasure to introduce our next presenter, Dr. Penny Policy. Dr. Policy holds degrees in Medicine and in Law from Harvard and is an advisor to the non-profit Bipartisan Connection. She has written extensively on healthcare reform and decision making by doctors and others in the trenches. Penny, take it away.

Dr. Policy: Thanks, Paul. It's a pleasure to join such

a distinguished faculty for this meeting. Dr. Pender has touched on healthcare reform in his chapter on Review of Systems, so I won't attempt to cover the same ground. However, the take-home points I suggest will allow meeting attendees to better understand the stakes involved as we attempt to rebuild trust in healthcare.

Policy wonks come in all sizes, from all backgrounds, and some are even physicians. The late Dr. Tom Coburn, former US Senator from Oklahoma, continued to see his OB/GYN patients when Congress was not in session. He was challenged for practicing medicine on the side when he should have been legislating. Stupid, right? You can't always make sense of what Congress decides to do, especially when it comes to something so personal as healthcare. A version of Obamacare was Teddy Kennedy's dream, and his terminal illness sparked a movement to pass some form of national health insurance before his death. John McCain also suffered the terminal effects of a brain tumor as a sitting US Senator. One of his final votes was to defeat a measure to repeal Obamacare served up by Senate Republicans. The reach and cost of Obamacare were not clearly appreciated when it was passed a decade ago. What we are seeing now is how a dysfunctional healthcare system, one that covered healthcare for the insured, is causing premiums for them and the newly insured to skyrocket. One writer posed a pertinent question regarding the source of healthcare reform.[101] "Is a more efficient healthcare system to be had by empowering just the right MIT professor to back his theories with government mandates, or by empowering market mechanisms to channel the choices of millions of consumers from the bottom up?"

The emphasis on value to replace volume for how doctors are paid has a strong foothold in federal programs, such as Medicare and Medicaid. The problem with continuing the status quo is that we will go broke. These entitlement programs are unsustainable in current form. Changes are sure to come, but what changes will be signed into law remains a question for legislators, lobbyists and healthcare activists. What we seem to want to preserve is employer-sponsored health insurance, regardless of what happens to the entitlement programs. Unfortunately, doctors who participate with Medicare and Medicaid will continue to see their fees shrink. A federal plan, to collapse the Evaluation and Management codes to just a few categories that physicians and other providers depend on for billing their services, demonstrates the desperation of some in Congress to apply the brakes to healthcare spending. The election of 2020 had been slated as a referendum on the economy and its masters; now the focus is on how the pandemic was handled and how the recovery will be judged. Healthcare is not only an election issue this year; what shape healthcare reform takes will affect us for years to come. Peter Martin, an attorney specializing in healthcare issues and who represents non-profit organizations, suggests in his firm's newsletter that we can expect a permanent expansion of the scope of practice of limited-license practitioners that was temporarily instituted during the pandemic.[102] The insult to our economy from the shutdown and its implications for those losing health insurance is analyzed in a position paper from *Health Management*.[103] The article describes how unemployment affects the uninsured rates. Estimates for the effects of low, moderate and high unemployment are given. There is greater impact for the unemployed from those states that did not elect to participate in Medicaid expansion as part of Obamacare. The Consolidated Omnibus Budget Reconciliation Act (COBRA) may provide a temporary safety net, but losing a job forces a hunt, not only for a new job, but also for new health insurance when COBRA benefits expire.

Right now, I would describe our situation as chaotic. If physicians hope to play a key role in the next wave of healthcare reform, they need to show the decision-makers a better way to deliver care. The coronavirus crisis created a window for action. It's now or never for doctors to lead the way.

Dr. Pender: Thanks, Penny. Next time, tell us what you really think! Seriously, you raise the important concept of physician leadership to rebuild trust in healthcare. We will return to that subject later in the meeting. Next, I would like to invite Dr. Sheryl Social to give us some perspective on our interactions, both professional and personal, before and after the pandemic. Dr. Social teaches a course at Yale on the society's response to stress. Sheryl, the floor is yours.

Dr. Social: Thank you for inviting me to present my subject in 5 minutes or less, Paul! (Laughter) I usually take a semester to cover the subject, but I will summarize my research and place my conclusions in a contemporary context of trust.

Patterns of behavior that lead to engagement are part of our make-up as human beings. For physicians, the doctor's lounge had been a place to meet colleagues, to discuss difficult cases, and to grab a donut before making rounds in the hospital. In his *Atlantic* paper, Dr. Richard Gunderman[104] asked the question, "What Happened to the Doctors' Lounge?" As the demands of time for patient care increased, the attendance in the lounge decreased. For hospitals, repurposing the spaces that had been reserved for private conversations was a financial necessity. Doctors' lounges were abandoned, forcing the closure of one of the prime locations for meeting physicians new to the medical staff. The decision was just one factor in creating feelings of isolation among physicians. Before the pandemic, as you heard Paul discuss in the Social History portion of his case presentation, the issue of burnout had become prominent in the literature. Now that we have seen the worst of the pandemic, what scars have been left on society? Recent articles in the lay press describe the subject of mourning our dead and the toll it has taken on doctors and patients alike.[105] Dr. Cacciatore's quote captures the feelings of his fellow physicians. "At some point this pandemic will end. But grief doesn't end. Right now, we need what we have always needed but have never been able to muster as a society: unrestricted compassion." Jill Lapore, a history professor at Harvard, has written about the parables associated with pandemics.[106] She positions people on rungs of a ladder of civilization, capable of moving up or down, depending on conditions. When stressed to the extreme, as when confronted with a plague, we may degenerate into tribal warfare, violence and destruction of the human spirit. Lapore cites the work of Jose Saramago, a Nobel Laureate, in *Blindness*,[107] where suddenly everyone loses vision. The hero is the wife of an ophthalmologist who leads the afflicted as the sole person who can see. The survivors' eyesight returns just as unexpectedly after a foray to a church. The lesson here is that in times of stress, we have to learn to trust each other, to look out for each other, and have faith that better times are ahead. One final word on the isolation of the sick and dying during the pandemic. With improved testing, families should be able to spend time with their loved one in their last days. Whether the illness is COVID-19, cancer, chronic obstructive pulmonary disease, or whatever, our humanity demands a final farewell that is personal, not virtual. No one should have to die alone. [108]

Dr. Pender: Sheryl, we really appreciate your insights into the human condition, especially in difficult times like these.

Now I would like to move into the subject of America's financial condition as we begin to emerge from the coronavirus pandemic. The challenge to hospitals, to businesses and to medical practices is profound. To address these issues, in the context of rebuilding trust in healthcare, is our next presenter. Dr. Frank Finance is a nationally recognized economist in the field of healthcare systems. Frank, thanks for your participation.

Dr. Finance: No problem, Paul. I am seeing Zoom meetings in my sleep! What makes this one different is that at the end of the session, we should have a roadmap for rebuilding trust in healthcare, or so I hope. It is curious that Wall Street is ahead of the trust curve right now.[109] Consumer sentiment lags as it usually does after a recession. However, the injury suffered by the economy may be more short-lived than previous recessions, compared to damage caused, for example, by the savings and loan debacle of the 1990s or by the sub-prime mortgage toxin experienced in the financial crisis of 2008. The stock market reflects anticipation of future events, while society attempts to make do with the current conditions. The federal government's handling of the payments to hospitals got off to a bit of a clumsy start as these were tied to historical Medicare levels of reimbursement, rather than to the actual costs of COVID treatment.[110] Corrections were made in subsequent payment mechanisms, but hospitals may continue to hurt financially. A lot of their revenue depends on diagnostic testing and elective surgical procedures that ground to a halt during the shutdown.[111] The healthcare plans that pay for many of those procedures are commercial or employer-based. That was the financial cushion for hospitals. Unfortunately, while hospitals are waiting for elective surgical volumes to resume, they face Medicare payments for COVID care that just meet their costs to deliver that care, and they experience bottom lines depleted by services to Medicaid recipients and the uninsured. It is not a formula for success as the economy opens up.

Has the bottom arrived yet? Economists are great at a retrospective view but not so great when predicting the future. An analysis from Merrill Lynch looked at five factors that must be met before economic vitality can be restored.[112] In summary, these are gradually being satisfied since the April 2020 writing of the article.

What about the recovery of medical practices? Taking your specialty as an example, Paul, ophthalmologists were surveyed by the American Academy of Ophthalmology regarding their level of activity.[113] The professional organization received 2,500 responses to their questions, and the results are likely representative of many medical practices. "Three-quarters of U.S. ophthalmologists say they have started scheduling patients for routine or elective care, while two-thirds are starting to resume surgery, according to the Academy's latest member pulse survey. However, reopening is a slow process." For patients to return to their rescheduled appointments, they must trust that their doctors are safely applying guidelines that reduce the chance of coronavirus transmission.

Dr. Pender: We appreciate your comments, Frank, especially with regard to the bond of trust between doctors and patients going forward. Our next presenter, Dr. Tammy Tech, is the youngest woman ever named full professor of computer science at Stanford. She teaches a course at the medical school as part of the curriculum for advanced analytics in medicine. I am delighted to introduce my good friend, and mentor on all things digital. Tammy, the floor is yours.

Dr. Tech: Thanks, Paul. The short version of what I have to say is that what you think you know about the future of medical care has yet to be imagined. The applications we use today to extract data on a periodic basis will be replaced with live streaming of personal health information that will monitor chronic conditions. Patient interfaces on mobile devices will allow for near immediate health advice from physicians through telemedicine. The range of technology available to doctors and patients will boggle your mind. Think about the rapid exchange of information among healthcare workers while battling the pandemic.[114] "Health care workers are writing the playbook for treating coronavirus patients on the fly, knowing they can't wait for *peer-reviewed articles or studies* in established medical journals. Instead they are tapping into social media, podcasts, inside-baseball medical blogs and text-message groups to share improvised solutions to supply shortages and patient care, forcing hospitals to quickly reevaluate their practices."

Collaboration among professionals is necessary when time is limited and lives are at stake. Technology facilitates the urgent needs of doctors to get information right away. As the population ages, and as the medical conditions requiring treatment expand, doctors will look toward the most efficient means to achieve that information. Furthermore, once treatment has been instituted, reminders will become commonplace on patients' mobile devices. Gone will be the office brochures that get discarded anyway. Follow-up loops will be programmed into the visit to ensure adherence to recommendations. One such company has developed the technology to improve both compliance and satisfaction from patients.[115]

Tech/Information Management	
Old	**New**
Programming	Configuration
Subject Matter Experts	Business rules
Version Control/Testing	Real time change
Separate systems/data	Simple integrated system

Courtesy of Vxtra Health

Trust in healthcare will be rebuilt from patient engagement, and technology will become an intimate partner in the process.

Dr. Pender: Thanks so much, Tammy, for giving us a glimpse of the future of technology and how it will impact the trust patients have in physicians. Next on our meeting agenda is an update on therapeutics from Dr. Mark Medications, who holds degrees in pharmacology and bioethics. Mark, you are good to go.

Dr. Medications: Thanks for inviting me, Paul. My remarks will be brief, since we have so few therapies for COVID-19. As far as treatment, the most promising drug, in the absence of a vaccine to prevent the infection in the first place, is remdesivir from Gilead Sciences, Inc. A press release from the company reported early success in shortening the duration of hospital stays when the drug is administered intravenously. The mechanism of action seems to interfere with the ability of the coronavirus to replicate.

Research centers and community hospitals are all clamoring for access to remdesivir, now that the FDA has given approval for emergency use. It remains in limited supply, which leads me to the next topic. How do we distribute a limited amount of the drug that may prove lifesaving?

Medical ethicists struggle with the concept of musical chairs, where some unlucky souls are just not able to grab a seat when the music stops. Various approaches have been cited by groups of doctors and healthcare executives for making available a scarce resource. Methods include a lottery, first-come first-served and distribution by proportion of those most affected, namely those whose health disparities caused them the greatest incidence of disease. There is no right answer to this dilemma. The subject of ethical treatment arose when the anticipated supply of ventilators was less than the demand. Going beyond advanced age as a consideration for not offering this potential lifesaver, some advocated for a profile of characteristics. Would having Alzheimer's disease exclude the patient from consideration for intubation and ventilation? Doctors and families face difficult decisions every day for maintaining quality of life in the face of grave odds for recovery. Advance directives for what measures the patient prefers help lead the discussion, but not every critically ill patient has expressed such preferences in writing. Often, the family member turns to the doctor and says, "If this were your mother, what would you do?" That ethical burden comes with the territory for physicians and their care teams.

COVID-19 is a challenge because more organs than the lungs are involved in the most serious cases. In the absence of some modulating factor, our immune cells, namely T-lymphocytes, become activated by the virus and set up a cascade of responses resulting in damage to tissues. The tissue targeted—lung, brain, kidney or other site—shows cells damaged as innocent bystanders to the chain reaction caused by cytokines, chemical mediators of the immune response. Expanded studies with tocilizumab are ongoing to find the best ways to blunt the cytokine storm.

Some good news comes from a large UK study[116] of dexamethasone, a steroid to combat inflammation in patients on ventilators. This cheap and widely available drug cut deaths by one-third among patients critically ill with COVID-19. The data are compelling for using this drug to alter the body's response to cytokines. The drug did not alter the clinical course of those infected with coronavirus who had only mild symptoms. Dr. Fauci explained why this drug should work in extreme conditions:

"When you're so far advanced that you're on a ventilator, it's usually that you have an aberrant or hyperactive inflammatory response that contributes as much to the morbidity and mortality as any direct viral effect."

Before I close my remarks, just a word on antibodies. We are trying to determine if prior exposure to the coronavirus, either from a common cold or other variants, provides some long-lasting protection for individuals, particularly children. The observation that young patients have less morbidity and mortality from COVID infection than older patients may give some credence to the theory. Why are men more likely to die from the infection than women? We don't know enough about sex differences in immune systems to come to any conclusions.

Finally, there is also some good news about antibody tests.[117] Roche Holding AG, the Swiss drug maker, announced that the FDA granted emergency use for their test. It was 100% accurate for indicating the presence of antibodies to coronavirus, and 99.8% accurate for ruling out those antibodies. In other words, only 2 cases out of 1,000 samples lacking the antibodies would show a "false-positive" result. Such tests would give a more complete picture of the extent of infection in the population. It is estimated that around 60% of the population would need antibodies to establish "herd immunity," whereby the virus can't easily find access to a host before being neutralized. Questions remain whether having antibodies would prevent reinfection. The notion of issuing return to work "passports" to people carrying antibodies is conjecture at the moment. Stay tuned.

Dr. Pender: Thanks, Mark, for the update. I would emphasize to our attendees that the opinions expressed are those of the individuals and not necessarily those of their parent institutions. Furthermore, the information is current as of mid-June 2020.

Before I introduce our next speaker, I would like to refer you to a video interview with Arthur C. Brooks of Harvard Business School and the Kennedy School of Government.[118] The series, *Managing Through Crisis*, features faculty members who help to develop leaders in government, business and non-profit organizations. Brooks offers ways in which we can remain positive in the face of distress from COVID-19. The tease for the interview states, "Social distancing and being forced to work remotely due to the coronavirus has us feeling a range of emotions every day, from happy or sad, to anxious, nervous, disconnected, and sometimes even grief." One tip Brooks mentions is to make eye contact, even if your connection is virtual. When I look back on the trust I shared with my patients, Brooks' comment on how the hormone oxytocin is generated in such exchanges made sense. Eye contact and touch are what drive the "love" hormone, the chemical mediator that allows us to want to give up our lives for that newborn baby, the one who will make lots of noise and demand our complete attention. With social distancing, it becomes harder, but looking directly at the person during a telehealth visit will improve the bond with that patient.

Brooks goes on to discuss what leaders must do in a crisis to improve morale in their organizations, a consideration that directly applies to physicians and their practices. It is not helpful to simply say everything will be just fine. Being hopeful, rather than optimistic, is what Brooks stresses. Among the possibilities are recovery as well as ruin, and we just don't know how things will eventually work out. However, we will remain strong and hopeful that we can find solutions to our situation. Those who follow look for signs that the leader is purposeful and determined in setting realistic goals, that is, someone worthy of leadership. Brooks' message of hope resonates with me.

Our next presenter has distinguished herself in executive leadership positions throughout her career in medicine. Mentoring students and residents while serving as managing partner for a large medical practice, Dr. Leslie Leadership has gained a reputation for integrity, administrative expertise, and intellectual curiosity. Leslie, thanks for accepting my invitation to present your thoughts.

Dr. Leadership: Thanks for the invitation to speak at a meeting with such an impressive faculty! As I listened to Paul's case presentation on distrust in healthcare, I was reminded of historical precedent for crisis management in America. I, too, have read Professor McClay's book *Land of Hope*. The historian describes how Franklin D. Roosevelt dealt with the Great Depression America was facing when he gave his inauguration speech in 1933. He honestly acknowledged the extent of the nation's problems and yet provided hope that they could be solved:

"I assume unhesitatingly the leadership of this great army of our people," and we shall be "treating the task as we would treat the emergency of a war." As McClay states prophetically, "it would remain to be seen whether that idea would fare better now than it had before—and what casualties this particular war might produce." You could say the same about the effect of the pandemic on America. The casualties were not only the deaths from coronavirus; among them were trust in our healthcare system. Fear of the unknown and suspicion sown online have brought us all a feeling of unease. In such times we look to leaders for guidance. Drs. Fauci and Birx provided needed leadership as the public health crisis emerged. We must also look to leaders across the political spectrum as the economy reopens. We must avoid a mindset of "us versus them." For earning our trust, leaders will get down in the trenches with us to show their concern and to rally the troops of their respective organizations.

On my office wall, I have a plaque with the words of a famous leader. Before I sit down to my computer to check my inbox, I silently speak those words to myself as a reminder of my role in my practice. *"The origin of great leadership begins with the respect of the commander for his subordinates."* —John Schofield, superintendent West Point, 1879. In that year, women were not commanders of troops, but the message still rings true today. Respect and trust are earned. You have to show by example your willingness to work so that others are inspired to follow.

I was recently sent an online opinion piece from a business executive who follows what CEOs are doing for their teams in a time of crisis. The gist of the article was that taking action is necessary but not sufficient to lead. You have to engage everyone in the organization in order to succeed.[119] According to Gary Burnison of Korn Ferry, an international consulting firm, leaders must follow these six steps for crisis management:

1) Anticipate—predicting what lies ahead

2) Navigate—course correcting in real time

3) Communicate—continually

4) Listen—to what you don't want to hear

5) Learn—learning from experience to apply in the future

6) Lead—improve yourself to elevate others

His opinion piece was not just another collection of bullet points for subordinates. It spoke to the characteristics of leaders that people look up to. As physician leaders of healthcare teams, we must not lose sight of the defining element of our mission—patient-centered care. We will meet that mission by offering support, consistency and vision to our organizations. We can work to replace uncertainty with acceptable risk among the healthcare workers we lead.

Life goes on, and we must continue living and put fear aside if we want to maintain our humanity. As a physician, I have seen the effects, physical and psychological, of damage to our capacity as humans. Acting smartly and safely will get us through this mess, and we will be stronger for it.

Dr. Pender: That was inspirational, Leslie. Your presentation is the perfect segue to our next speaker, Dr. Victor Vxtra, CEO and Chief Medical Officer of Vxtra Health. His mission is to take back healthcare by empowering physicians to exercise their roles as patient advocates and to practice patient-centered healthcare. Contrary to the comment I recently heard from a fellow physician, "That ship has sailed," Vic has formed a company that is agile, smart, and may even divert the course of that healthcare vessel leaving port. Victor, you have the floor.

Dr. Vxtra: Thanks, Paul. I've enjoyed the comments from your presenters and hope to add to the discussion. We have worked closely with physician practices and have developed significant relationships with payers and hospitals in the South. Our medical advisory board has taken the lead to establish best practices for primary and specialty care across the medical spectrum. Doctor-led teams of distinction are the driving force behind our company. They are the early adopters of the disruption in healthcare following the pandemic. What I find most satisfying is that there is common ground among doctors to emerge from this healthcare crisis and to find ways to deliver better care at an attractive price. Working with employers and their benefits managers, Vxtra Health has created a win-win-win for the employers, the employees and the physicians who care for them. Our network of physicians combines local talent with accountability for outcomes. All members of the healthcare team are subject to peer review for quality care. Paul, in your previous discussion of Review of Systems, you mentioned Marty Makary, MD, and his group at Johns Hopkins. By studying physician practice patterns, they have been able to define what patterns and ranges are acceptable and what procedures and billings may be outliers. Taking the opinions of those in academic medicine and in clinical medicine, Makary and colleagues are applying data to policy development. The result for Vxtra Health is the elimination of prior authorization as a delaying tactic of payers. Trust in our company is built from the integrity of doctors, looking both in the mirror and toward their peers for what is appropriate care. Partnering with hospitals, insurance brokers, pharmacy benefits coordinators and an array of concierge services to engage the employee/patient, our company is taking the steps necessary to reconfigure healthcare.

It is said that the highest form of flattery is imitation. Other healthcare networks may claim to be patient-centered, but they run on outdated software and depend on opaque practices to maintain profitability. Vxtra Health takes the position that transparency is the disinfectant that the patient requires to make informed decisions. When patients trust their doctors and, by extension, their teams of distinction, they will achieve better service and health outcomes. Ours is a patient-driven economy, and Vxtra Health is making the experience for the patient extraordinary.

Dr. Pender: Thanks for your analysis, Vic. We have run out of time for questions for the panelists. But you know there will be much more to discuss on the subject of rebuilding trust in healthcare. That concludes our meeting for today.

Conclusion

THANKS FOR ATTENDING the Zoom meeting on Rebuilding Trust in Healthcare. Although it was a fictional exercise designed to pull together a range of ideas and opinions on the subject, it has served its purpose.

What I have learned since working with Larry Hightower, CEO of Vxtra Health, is that there *is* a way for physicians to re-establish their influence for serving their patients' needs. A focusing on patient-centered care will give doctors and their teams the autonomy to make decisions in the best interest of their patients. A healthcare system that understands what doctors do best and supports their calling as healers is also most beneficial to patients. Development of technology that is also patient-centered will be more efficient and result in better care at a better price. Vxtra Health is committed to enhancing patient-centered care and the patient-doctor relationship, demonstrating a model for other companies to follow. A company spokesperson has said, "we are the iPhone version when other healthcare networks are the flip phone version." And we now know how that played out.

Healthcare is a very personal matter, and it should be tailored to individuals, rather than forcing a bureaucratic, "one-size-fits-all" healthcare system on everyone. Rebuilding trust in healthcare is possible if the patient-physician relationship is the starting point for a new model of care. Respecting that bond allows trust to blossom, even in the face of a healthcare crisis like the coronavirus pandemic.

Summary

SO THERE YOU HAVE IT. I have completed my story, for the present time at least. The need to rebuild trust in healthcare should be apparent, and the direction I have chosen in which to nudge the process will hopefully have some positive impact. I would like to conclude with an image that has recurred in the course of my career as a physician: thoughts in the middle of the night that require my urgent attention.

An idea for my writing prompted me to get up, to grab my phone from its charger, and to go into the bathroom so as not to wake my wife. I entered in my notes "Billy Joel A Matter of Trust." I tried going back to sleep, but to no avail. I kept tossing and turning, thinking that over thirty years ago I had admired the songwriter's lyrics and music. Try as I might, I had trouble coming up with the lyrics. The music was in my head, though, including the chord progressions. I finally got out of bed at 5 am and finished my breakfast quickly. I quietly tiptoed to the study and booted up my laptop to search for the "official" video of *A Matter of Trust*[120], produced in 1986.

As I watched the video and listened with my earphones, I felt like a parable for my message of rebuilding trust was unfolding before my eyes and ears. The production was cleverly set in a simulation of a residential block in the Bronx resembling Billy Joel's birth home. The artist began his song with his band but stopped the performance after a few measures. "It's too hot in here," was the device the producer used to allegedly make the band members open the windows for ventilation, but it was really done to blast the performance into a crowded street. The set cameras swept a collection of New Yorkers, first as just curious passersby, then ultimately as participants in the rock music being performed inside the apartment. The lyrics brought tears to my eyes as I absorbed the dual messages of getting over deceit and missed connections, and of the hope of developing trust in a new relationship. The rollicking residents recalled for me past images of the Big Apple as a source of diversity, spontaneity and immense energy. A contrary voice from the third-floor fire escape yelled, "SHUT UP!" The performance featured a cameo of Joel's wife, Christie Brinkley the supermodel, looking radiant with their young child as they moved among the band members. Their marriage wasn't to last. Joel divorced and remarried multiple times. He is obviously a brilliant songwriter and musician, among the most gifted artists of his generation. Like many famous artists, however, his depression and substance abuse nearly took his life. Looking back 34 years to his video, I was taken by the power of his music and the poignancy of his lyrics. The idea of commitment to everlasting love is scary, and people have been burned in the past. But as a matter of trust, let's see how we do.

As we emerge from our caves to face our post-pandemic world, it feels like we have been released from witness protection to face an unfamiliar environment. The threat still exists, and we must guard against complacency. For New York and its feeder populations, the epicenter of the pandemic, it will take longer than most cities to recover before people can enjoy the expressions of freedom depicted in that music video of a generation before. We look forward to jamming together once again, just like the extras in that Billy Joel production.

Perhaps that is how we should proceed with healthcare reform, with hope for the future. As we rebuild trust, the form healthcare takes may morph into something better than we could have imagined. Without question, we have endured both the internal and external adverse effects on the patient-doctor relationship. Fortunately, medicine should remain a noble profession if physicians maintain a level of honesty, compassion and skill with their patients. That should be the basis for healthcare reform, and all the rest should be an outgrowth of that relationship.

Afterword

AS THIS BOOK WAS GOING TO PRESS, a health benefits management company went public. Accolade (ACCD on the Nasdaq exchange) submitted the requisite S-1 form to the Securities and Exchange Commission for an Initial Public Offering. Essentially, the company leverages the expertise of nurses and other clinicians to answer questions that employees have about their health plan. But how exactly does Accolade do this? A careful reading of the Accolade prospectus reveals "we do not provide medical care or establish patient relationships with our members." In other words, Accolade is charging employers for advice, not clinical care. What are the implications? Is this real reform? Why or why not? Shouldn't the actual care members receive be part of the solution? Connect with me on paulpendermd.com. Let's all work together on a solution that works for patients, physicians and policy makers.

Endnotes

[1] Pender, P. LinkedIn, January 4, 2019

[2] https://journals.lww.com/academicmedicine/Fulltext/2017/01000/Educating_for_the_21st_Century_Health_Care_System_.16.aspx

[3] https://www.cancernetwork.com/news/fda-approves-phase-iii-clinical-trial-tocilizumab-covid-19-pneumonia

[4] https://jamanetwork.com/journals/jama/fullarticle/2764727

[5] https://apnews.com/1ca088a5598032425796 30f88b99b681

[6] https://www.harvardmacy.org/index.php/hmi-courses/assessment

[7] https://www.wsj.com/articles/sweden-is-a-viral-punching-bag-11586905784?mod=opinion_featst_pos1

[8] https://www.wsj.com/articles/new-york-is-the-epicenter-of-the-world-11585869852?mod=hp_opin_pos_2

[9] https://journals.sagepub.com/doi/abs/10.1177/0046958-018759174

[10] https://www.ncbi.nlm.nih.gov/pmc/articles/PMC6183652/

[11] https://www.linkedin.com/pulse/burdens-burnout-paul-pender-md/?trackingId=t0OgITzaiUgMsue9Zy5h7A%3D%3D

[12] https://www.washingtonpost.com/opinions/why-doctors-quit/2015/05/28/1e9d8e6e-056f-11e5-a428-c984eb077d4e_story.html

[13] https://www.kevinmd.com/blog/2019/07/a-physician-writes-for-catharsis.html

[14] *The Power of the Personal Essay in Health Policy*. Narrative Matters. (Foreword). Johns Hopkins University Press 2006.

[15] https://www.ted.com/speakers/abraham_verghese?-language=en

[16] https://journals.sagepub.com/doi/abs/10.1177/1355819-614543161

[17] https://www.wsj.com/articles/young-doctors-struggle-to-treat-coronavirus-patients-we-are-horrified-and-scared-11588171553?mod=searchresults&page=1&pos=1

[18] https://www.statnews.com/2020/04/24/call-people-covid-19-positive-lessons-learned/

[19] https://m.facebook.com/1163771366/posts/102216369-82051547/

[20] https://www.aao.org/headline/coronavirus-kills-chinese-whistleblower-ophthalmol

[21] https://www.wsj.com/articles/world-health-coronavirus-disinformation-11586122093?mod=searchresults&page=1&pos=1

22 https://www.newyorker.com/magazine/2020/05/04/what-the-corona-virus-crisis-reveals-about-american-medicine

23 https://www.documentcloud.org/documents/4614406-Medical-Board-Decision.html

24 https://www.latimes.com/local/lanow/la-me-ln-usc-dean-medical-license-20180720-story.html

25 Diagnostic and Statistical Manual of Mental Disorders (DSM-5), 2013

26 https://pagepressjournals.org/index.php/qrmh/issue/-view/634in volume 3, p 121-124, Feb 16, 2020

27 https://www.wsj.com/articles/one-medical-injustice-corrected-11583526869

28 https://www.kevinmd.com/blog/2020/04/please-make-the-tragic-death-of-this-physician-mean-something.html

29 https://www.kevinmd.com/blog/2019/11/parallel-thinking-wont-solve-problems-in-health-care.html

30 Duckworth, A. *Grit: The Power of Passion and Perseverance*. Scribner, 2016

31 https://www.hks.harvard.edu/faculty-research/policy-topics/democr-acy-governance/nancy-gibbs-truth-and-trust

32 Brooks, A C. *Love Your Enemies: How Decent People Can Save America From the Culture of Contempt*. The American Enterprise Institute, 2019

33 Ibid

34 https://www.kevinmd.com/blog/2019/05/the-effect-of-mobile-devices-on-our-collective-psyche.html

35 https://michigantoday.umich.edu/2020/04/23/the-perils-of-social-media-and-self-delusion/

36 Tolentino, J. *Trick Mirror: Reflections on Self-Delusion*. Random House, 2019

37 Carreyrou, J. *Bad Blood: Secrets and Lies in a Silicon Valley Startup*. Vantage Books, 2018

38 https://www.linkedin.com/pulse/prudent-layperson-standard-should-apply-urgent-care-paul-pender-md/?trackingId=FN3P9WzMJ7aZLUS%2BlDDUlA%3D%3D

39 http://newsroom.acep.org/2017-06-09-prudent-layperson-standard

40 https://innovaccer.com/media/session-presentation/covid-optimism.pdf/?redirect=false

41 https://www.ama-assn.org/practice-management/sustainability/covid-19-epicenter-breaking-silos-led-better-teamwork

42 https://www.wsj.com/articles/floridas-pioneering-medical-reforms-11585694842

43 https://www.issuelab.org/resources/22899/22899.pdf

44 Ibid

45 https://www.wsj.com/articles/a-top-immunologist-on-why-corona-virus-is-killing-more-african-americans-11587556800?mod=hp_lead_pos10

46 Ibid

47 https://www.ama-assn.org/press-center/press-releases/ama-outlines-ambitious-approach-toward-health-equity

48 https://www.ama-assn.org/about/leadership/why-racial-and-ethnic-data-covid-19-s-impact-badly-needed

49 https://www.nytimes.com/2020/04/07/opinion/coronavirus-blacks.html

50 https://suiteweb.atpointofcare.com/?token=7a43e3d51b3510461aefc5-4155a825d9&utm_source=7105&utm_campaign=516&utm_medium=email#library/news/breakingmed/82223

51 Hyman, M. *Food Fix: How to Save Our Health, Our Economy, Our Communities, and Our Planet—One Bite at a Time.* Little, Brown Spark, 2020

52 https://www.wsj.com/articles/new-york-citys-coronavirus-deaths-match-demographics-in-other-hot-spots-11587214800?emailToken=d2809bc49b19649aa7c78799bd624d41Zxx7An4+PxJFyYpi8BU5gLZwT5xQ4ajnai8EypX7EyQaMiSPdl4Bs2zsFaCA8By033vUUkgfDxr7L6xAz35Zv5ioOQonW3YtBpXTiGVBoIxJCzs0q1zn/QdyalESwKZQv8b6G9op5e/IZ02y58FG5w%3D%3D&reflink=article_email_share

53 NH Department of Health and Human Services, NH Institutions Associated with COVID-19 Outbreak, May 4, 2020

54 https://news.harvard.edu/gazette/story/2020/04/kevin-cranston-took-his-m-div-degree-to-bureau-of-public-health/

55 https://www.cdc.gov/coronavirus/2019-ncov/downloads/ community/workplace-decision-tree.pdf

56 https://www.foxnews.com/media/matthew-mcconaughey-coronavirus-divisions-politicization.amp

57 https://www.aao.org/member-services/member-obituaries-detail/richard-p-mills-md-mph

58 https://www.wsj.com/articles/coronavirus-deepens-millennials-feeling-they-cant-get-a-break-11587393262

59 Tolentino, J. *Trick Mirror*, Random House, 2019.

60 https://www.kevinmd.com/blog/2020/04/in-these-dark-times-of-a-pandemic-look-to-history-for-hope.html

61 https://www.cdc.gov/coronavirus/2019-ncov/downloads/ community/workplace-decision-tree.pdf

62 Mukherjee, S. *The Emperor of All Maladies.* Scribner, 2010

63 Ibid

[64] Ibid

[65] Brill, S. *America's Bitter Pill: Money, Politics, Backroom Deals, and the Fight to Fix Our Broken Healthcare System.* Random House, 2015

[66] Ibid

[67] Ibid

[68] jama_obama_2016_sc_160013.pdf

[69] Pipes, S. *False Premise, False Promise: The Disastrous Reality of Medicare for All.* Encounter Books, 2020

[70] Ibid.

[71] https://www.opensecrets.org/news/2020/01/lobbying-spending-in-2019-near-all-time-high/

[72] George, E. *Big Medicine: The Cost of Corporate Control and How Doctors and Patients Working Together Can Rebuild a Better System,* Alethos Press, 2015

[73] Ibid

[74] https://rxforsuccesspodcast.com/bonus-stop-the-kick-backs-with-dr-marion-mass/

[75] https://www.rand.org/health-care/key-topics/health-policy/in-depth.html

[76] https://bipartisanpolicy.org/wp-content/uploads/2020/01/BPC_2020-Health-Care-Presentation_Final.pdf

[77] Ibid

[78] Makary, M. *The Price We Pay: What Broke American Health Care and How to Fix It.* Bloomsbury Publishing, 2019

[79] Ibid

[80] https://dnyuz.com/2020/03/29/the-u-s-tried-to-build-a-new-fleet-of-ventilators-the-mission-failed/

[81] https://www.newyorker.com/magazine/2020/05/04/seattles-leaders-let-scientists-take-the-lead-new-yorks-did-not

[82] https://www.wsj.com/articles/health-chiefs-early-missteps-set-back-coronavirus-response-11587570514?mod=searchresults&page=1&pos=2

[83] https://www.newyorker.com/science/medical-dispatch/a-boston-hospital-nears-its-limits

[84] https://www.kevinmd.com/blog/2020/03/my-colleagues-are-nervous-my-patients-are-crying-and-yet-we-are-here.html

[85] https://dnyuz.com/2020/04/14/im-an-e-r-doctor-in-new-york-none-of-us-will-ever-be-the-same/

[86] https://www.newyorker.com/magazine/2020/04/20/how-anthony-fauci-became-americas-doctor

[87] https://www.kevinmd.com/blog/2020/04/truth-dies-in-silence-sadly-so-do-people.html

[88] https://www.facebook.com/NBAONTNT/videos/ernie-johnsons-message-before-the-match/879742102540250/

[89] McClay, W. *Land of Hope: An Invitation to the Great American Story*, Encounter Books, 2019

[90] https://www.wsj.com/articles/why-does-reopening-polarize-us-11589842995?mod=opinion_lead_pos5

[91] https://www.wsj.com/articles/experts-arent-enough-11589465220?-mod=searchresults&page=1&pos=1

[92] Mukherjee, S. *The Emperor of All Maladies*, Scribner, 2010

[93] https://www.ted.com/talks/laurel_braitman_the_mental_health-_benefits_of_storytelling_for_health_care_workers?language=en

[94] https://khn.org/news/beyond-burnout-docs-decry-moral-injury-from-financial-pressures-of-health-care/

[95] https://www.kevinmd.com/blog/2020/03/the-next-pandemic-will-be-in-mental-health.html

[96] https://www.kevinmd.com/blog/2020/04/an-oncologists-prescription-for-managing-fear-and-chaos-in-the-covid-19-pandemic.html

[97] https://www.statnews.com/2020/05/21/calling-health-care-workers-heroes-harms-all-of-us/

[98] https://www.kevinmd.com/blog/2020/05/it-took-a-pandemic-to-reveal-the-secret-health-care-workers.html

[99] https://www.wsj.com/articles/novartis-inks-deal-to-make-experiment-al-coronavirus-vaccine-11590702909

[100] https://jamanetwork.com/journals/jama/fullarticle/2764727

[101] https://www.wsj.com/articles/experts-arent-enough-11589465220?mod=searchresults&page=1&pos=1

[102] https://www.bowditch.com/2020/04/01/client-alert-cares-act-provis-ions-assisting-health-care-providers-response-to-the-pandemic/

[103] https://www.healthmanagement.com/wp-content/uploads/HMA-Estimates-of-COVID-Impact-on-Coverage-public-version-for-April-3-8 30-CT.pdf

[104] https://www.theatlantic.com/health/archive/2013/11/what-happened-to-the-doctors-lounge/281112/

[105] https://www.wsj.com/articles/sharing-the-rites-of-consolation-when-were-apart-11586531062?mod=hp_lista_pos1

[106] https://www.newyorker.com/magazine/2020/03/30/what-our-contagion-fables-are-really-about

[107] Saramago, J. *Blindness*. The Harvill Press, 1997

[108] https://www.wsj.com/articles/even-in-a-pandemic-no-one-should-have-to-die-alone-11586557751

[109] https://www.wsj.com/articles/the-stock-market-and-consumer-sentiment-are-telling-different-stories-11590571805

[110] https://suiteweb.atpointofcare.com/?token=7a43e3d51b3510461aefc54155a825d9&utm_source=7105&utm_campaign=519&utm_medium=email#library/news/breakingmed/82245

[111] https://www.wsj.com/articles/hospitals-face-difficult-recovery-from-coronavirus-crisis-11587483371?mod=searchresults&page=1&pos=2

[112] https://www.ml.com/articles/market-volatility/market-volatility-april-8-2020.recent.html

[113] https://www.aao.org/about/governance/academy-blog/post/survey-reopening-starts-slowly-ophthalmology

[114] https://www.wsj.com/articles/doctors-are-improvising-coronavirus-treatments-then-quickly-sharing-them-11586436031?mod=searchresults&page=1&pos=1

[115] https://www.patienteducationgenius.com

[116] https://www.nature.com/articles/d41586-020-01824-5

[117] https://www.wsj.com/articles/roche-coronavirus-antibody-test-wins-fda-approval-for-emergency-use-11588505019

[118] https://www.hbs.edu/news/articles/Pages/managing-through-crisis-how-to-be-happy.aspx?utm_source=SilverpopMailing&utm_medium=email&utm_campaign=Daily%20Gazette%2020200429%20(1)

[119] https://www.kornferry.com/insights/articles/burnison-coronavirus-leadership-crisis

[120] https://www.youtube.com/watch?v=6yYchgX1fMw.

Bibliography

Brill, S. *America's Bitter Pill: Money, Politics, Backroom Deals, and the Fight to Fix Our Broken Healthcare System*. Random House, 2015

Brooks, A.C. *Love Your Enemies: How Decent People Can Save America From the Culture of Contempt.* The American Enterprise Institute, 2019

Carreyrou, J. *Bad Blood: Secrets and Lies in a Silicon Valley Startup*. Vantage Books, 2018

Crenshaw, D. *Fortitude: American Resilience in the Era of Outrage*. Hatchette Book Group, Inc. 2020

Duckworth, A. *Grit: The Power of Passion and Perseverance*. Scribner, 2016

George, E. *Big Medicine: The Cost of Corporate Control and How Doctors and Patients Working Together Can Rebuild a Better System*. Alethos Press, 2015

Hyman, M. *Food Fix: How to Save Our Health, Our Economy, Our Communities, and Our Planet—One Bite at a Time*. Little, Brown Spark, 2020

Makary, M. *The Price We Pay: What Broke American Health Care and How to Fix It*. Bloomsbury Publishing, 2019

McClay, W. *Land of Hope: An Invitation to the Great American Story*, Encounter Books, 2019

Mukherjee, S. *The Emperor of All Maladies.* Scribner, 2010

Pipes, S. *False Premise, False Promise: The Disastrous Reality of Medicare for All.* Encounter Books, 2020

Saramago, J. *Blindness.* The Harvill Press, 1997

Tolentino, J. *Trick Mirror: Reflections on Self-Delusion.* Random House, 2019

About the Author

PAUL PENDER, MD, practiced clinical ophthalmology for 38 years, specializing in the medical and surgical treatment of eye diseases. He completed his residency at the world-renowned Wills Eye Hospital. Honors include a lecture series in his name by the New England Ophthalmological Society and the Secretariat Award from the American Academy of Ophthalmology for his work on webinars for clinicians. Paul is passionate about patient-centered care. He believes that the patient-physician relationship should serve as the fundamental building block for healthcare reform.

Dr. Pender blogs regularly on timely medical issues on his website **www.PaulPenderMD.com** and popular social media platforms. He is also an advisor to Vxtra Health, a company committed to collaborating with physicians to earn trust and manage healthcare costs.